# A SONG OF THEIR OWN

# A SONG OF THEIR OWN

## OF THEIR

## OWN

### THE FIGHT FOR VOTES FOR WOMEN IN IPSWICH

### JOY BOUNDS

The History Press

To all my friends in Ipswich Women's Festival Group

First published 2014

The History Press
The Mill, Brimscombe Port
Stroud, Gloucestershire, GL5 2QG
www.thehistorypress.co.uk

British Library Cataloguing in Publication Data.
A catalogue record for this book is available from the British Library.

ISBN 978 0 7509 5557 7

Typesetting and origination by The History Press
Printed in Great Britain

# CONTENTS

# ACKNOWLEDGEMENTS

**I**T WOULD BE impossible to thank every single person individually who has contributed towards this book. Writing a book can seem a rather lonely occupation, and yet every word is supported by the expertise, encouragement and help of others. What follows is an attempt to give a special mention to those whose input has been more significant.

Thanks to the women in the Ipswich Women's Festival Group, and its predecessor the Women's Local History Group. Their belief in the importance of women in the development of this town, and their desire to discover their actions and achievements, has been a great inspiration. We've had some good celebrations together too, including an event on the centenary of census night, April 1911.

The research for such a book as this would not be possible without the rich resource of libraries – and those resources would not be half so rich without the skill, dedication, knowledge and sheer helpfulness of their staff. Special thanks to Suffolk Record Office and The Women's Library (previously at the Metropolitan Library, and now at the London School of Economics). To a lesser extent, I'm also grateful to Girton College in Cambridge, and Colchester Museum for so willingly allowing me to access some of their material.

I was also fortunate to benefit from the generosity of others studying suffrage – particularly Jill Liddington and Ann Dingsdale. Thanks also to Nan Kerr for sharing with me a transcript of one of her interviews, and to Margaret Young of the Garrett family for her comments. Good friends Pat, Sue and Steve read early versions of my book, and their feedback was invaluable.

Finally, thanks are inadequate for the help and support of my son, Leif Dixon, who kept asking awkward questions, and was always ready with a handy piece of historical context. He has done his best to teach me to apply rigour to the puzzles, fragments and unanswerable questions thrown up by historical research.

# INTRODUCTION

[Women are] always a chorus joining in men's songs,
never allowed to sing a song of their own.

*Stowmarket suffrage meeting, 3 March 1911*

**P**EOPLE IN MANY countries across the world are still demanding the
right to vote and have a say in how their country is run. They want to
influence how the government makes its laws and spends their money,
and to have full citizenship. In contrast, Britain often congratulates itself on
being an 'old' democracy. Yet less than a century ago, within the lifetime of
many of our mothers or grandmothers, half the population of this country,
that is women, had no say in its government. In common with those other
people across the world, Britain's women were full of idealism, believing that
many of society's ills and inequalities would be cured if they had the vote.
They had to fight long and hard, against harsher opposition than could have
been expected, for over sixty years. It was only in 1918 that some women were
allowed to vote and another ten years, in 1928, before all women were granted
this right. However, democracy alone does not create equality, that is a goal we
have yet to achieve.

Like many people, I knew that this fight for the vote involved many years of
civil disobedience, imprisonment, hunger striking and forcible feeding. I knew
that the campaign became more bitter as the years went on; that some women's
health was affected; that protest changed into assault, criminal damage and
arson. However, I made the common assumption that these events occurred
in London and other big cities, orchestrated by women from large, influential
families like the Pankhursts and the Pethwick-Lawrences. I assumed that,
whilst individual women from other parts of the country might go and join in,
there was little organisation in the towns and villages of Britain – including
Ipswich in Suffolk, where I have lived throughout my adult life.

During the 1990s, I became interested in local women's history. I read about
early pioneers in various fields, and learnt that women in and around Ipswich
also fought for votes for women. In fact, I realised that the predominantly
London-based actions could not have been so successful, nor received so much
useful publicity, had the drive behind them not been supported in towns and

villages across the country. The vote was very hard won, and it was necessary to show continuously that the demand for it was widespread. Ipswich, it became apparent, had its own group of suffrage supporters, who held meetings to tell people how the entitlement to vote would enhance their lives, and who also mounted their own local actions. These actions sometimes meant that they suffered for their commitment.

Ipswich is a mid-sized county town, and whilst of course unique, it shares many similarities with other towns across the country. The response to the demand for votes for women was different in every town, but nevertheless, I hope that the story of the Ipswich women will add something of value to studies about what went on during the campaign outside of London.

To the best of my knowledge there are no books written about the suffragettes of the Ipswich area, though some of the stories are known as part of the town's history, and I felt there should be a record of their campaign. It was necessary to look for contemporary records of events which were mainly to be found in the local newspapers. There was also valuable information in the local reports within the national suffrage journals which I found in The Women's Library. This Library contains vital letters and minutes, as well as many other useful resources. There are, of course, hundreds of books written about the actions of suffragettes nationally, and these were an excellent source in increasing my understanding of the wider context in which the Ipswich women acted, and in helping me to make connections between all their experiences. Throughout the book, I have tried to explain what was happening locally against the backdrop of national politics and suffrage events.

Various themes arose from my reading and I was frequently struck by the courage and determination of these local women. At times when they held public meetings, the heckling was so loud, persistent and abusive that they could not get their message across, and had to give up. Sometimes the police had to break up meetings, and protect the women against possible and actual violence. For women who had little experience of public life, this must have been a terrifying experience. They had to train themselves to cope, and a picture emerges of a group of women empowering themselves over the years by their actions, and by supporting each other closely. Another striking theme was their idealism. For them, being able to vote was an overriding concern, but at the same time it was a means to other ends. Many of the local suffragettes had roles in other reforming organisations, showing particular concern for the conditions of working women, and the effects of poverty.

They felt that only when Parliament was truly representative of all the people, could conditions change. For them, there was a vital link between suffrage and social reform.

One question kept coming into my mind. Why did women have to fight so hard for such a basic, legitimate right? It is a complex issue, which I have tried to explore. What remains clear to me is that women's fight to have full equality in all aspects of life, and not to be identified with the domestic sphere alone, is encapsulated in this campaign, and remains a fight that is not yet over. Many men were, and still are, supportive of that aim.

Because of the extreme and highly controversial actions of the final years of the women's suffrage campaign (about 1911–14), which included serious criminal damage, arson and personal sacrifice, it can easily be forgotten that the fight for the vote had already been going on for the best part of half a century. It was in the mid-1860s that the first petition was presented to parliament requesting the vote for women on the same terms as men. This book starts at that point, and in Chapter One we look at how women from this area came to sign that petition. It was a time when women were beginning to resent their status as second-class citizens, and to demand access to higher education and to the professions. They wanted to have more rights over their money and property, and indeed over their children. These campaigns would go on for many years alongside, and beyond, the fight for the vote.

For a long time women across the country, including in and around Ipswich, met to talk about suffrage and what it would mean to have the vote. They held public meetings and lobbied their Members of Parliament. By the end of the century more men had been enfranchised, but still not a single woman could vote in a parliamentary election despite the support of a majority of MPs. It was then that the suffrage campaign changed dramatically. 'Deeds not Words' became its driving force, with new suffrage organisations creating more dynamic and controversial campaign tactics. How these ideas were reflected locally in the early years of the twentieth century is the subject of Chapters 2–6. Then, in Chapter 7, we see how East Suffolk was not exempt from the arson campaign, perhaps the most controversial of all the tactics of the militant suffragettes.

Finally, I have included as much information as possible about the individual, local women who were involved, as a tribute to their courage and commitment. Their idealism sings through their actions. It is obvious that they wanted a more just, equal society and that they cared passionately about women's working conditions, about poverty and about subservience in the home. They believed that if women had power and influence in and outside of the home, many of the country's problems could be solved. It is this desire to create a better future that connects these women with all those who now, and in previous times, right across the world, fight for justice for women and long for true equality.

# 1

# THE LADIES' PETITION 1866

## The long path to universal suffrage

In 1866, sixteen women from Ipswich signed the first ever petition asking parliament to grant them the vote. Nationally, the petition attracted 1,499 signatures. By today's standards this was very small – even by the end of the nineteenth century such petitions might attract half a million signatures – but during this period there were few women's organisations or societies campaigning for 'Votes for Women'. In fact we may wonder how a petition on such a topic was achieved in just a few weeks, with signatures from many places across the country.

At that time, no woman could vote in either a national or local election, or be elected to Parliament. The signatories of what became known as 'The Ladies' Petition' might have been horrified if they had known how long it would be before all women gained those rights – sixty-two years. It was only in 1928 that Britain could finally claim to be a full democracy, with a Parliament which was elected by both men and women.

By the time of that first petition in 1866, some men were enfranchised. The year 1832 had marked the first great Reform Act after years of agitation by both men and women. This Act established for the first time that the vote was not just for the richest landowners and most prominent men in society; it paved the way for the election of a wider cross section of politicians from the industrial cities. Even so, the electorate only rose slightly from 435,000 to 650,000 voters – about 7 per cent of the population. Women were disappointed to be excluded, since they were increasingly active in public life. Educated, middle-class women sat on local Health and School Boards, and were involved in the social development of their areas.

The limited enfranchisement of men soon led to more radical action, with the Chartists[*] demonstrating, petitioning and agitating for further reform. The newly formed trade unions, Friendly Societies and Co-operative Movement, in which women were also active, fought to show that working people were 'deserving' of the vote. Chartism was not as strong in Suffolk as in the industrialised North, but even so, in the late 1830s, thousands of people packed into Ipswich Town Hall to hear about the Charter, followed by large meetings in Suffolk's smaller towns and villages.[1]

It was within the context of this growing pressure for further reform that some women decided to be more specific about their need for suffrage. During the recent 1865 general election campaign there had been talk of further enfranchisement of men, and women wanted to be part of it. They were encouraged by the election of supportive MPs like Henry Fawcett and John Stuart Mill, who had mentioned issues of women's suffrage in his election address.[2]

## The Petition

The Ladies' Petition was instigated by the Kensington Society, a debating society in London set up in 1865 by a group of middle-class women who specifically wanted to increase opportunities for women. It grew out of Langham Place, a club where unaccompanied women could go to rest and get something to eat, and where there were various meetings and events. The campaigning *English Woman's Journal* was published from there. Some of the most radical women of the time were members of both the Langham Place Group and the Kensington Society. These were women who were already leading action on women's inequality in society or who would later do so. Their leader was Barbara Bodichon (*née* Leigh-Smith), a dynamic woman who with another member, Emily Davies, was campaigning for women's access to further education. Other members were Suffolk's Elizabeth Garrett, who had fought to become a doctor, and her older sister, Louisa.

Educated, able and ambitious women had very few opportunities at this time. The professions were closed to them and, because women could not access higher education, they could not become properly qualified to teach, or progress beyond being governesses. A number of women were carers or nurses but it was not until 1860 that Florence Nightingale would start to train nurses and bring

---

[*] The People's Charter 1838 demanded universal suffrage. Chartism was a working-class movement fighting for political reform.

**ELIZABETH GARRETT ANDERSON** (1836–1917), as she became known on her marriage in 1871, came to live in Aldeburgh, Suffolk as a child. Her life spanned the whole period of women's fight for the vote – she died just a year before the first women were enfranchised. Her father, Newson Garrett, was a successful businessman and maltster, and built up his coal and coke business at the complex of buildings which now includes the famous Snape Maltings Concert Hall. His grandfather had founded the successful agricultural machinery works at Leiston.

Newson Garrett was unusual in that he wanted his daughters to be educated, and five of the six were sent away to school. However, afterwards there was nothing to do but return home and await a suitable marriage. Elizabeth's letters to her friend Emily Davies, who unlike her brothers had not been allowed to go to school at all, show her immense frustration with her life. In 1859, she decided she wanted to become a doctor. She had to fight hard against her parents to achieve her ambition, although they fully supported her later.

As a woman, she was unable to gain acceptance to any English medical school, and therefore trained as a nurse at a Middlesex hospital. Discovering that the Society of Apothecaries did not ban women from taking their medical exams, she did so and, in 1865, was awarded the certificate which enabled her to practice as a doctor.[*] So she became the first woman doctor trained in England. Throughout her long professional life, she was active in developing the treatment of women's ill-health.

Elizabeth Garrett Anderson achieved many other successes in her life, from which women would long continue to benefit. Her story is interesting, not only because it is that of a Suffolk woman who with others instigated and signed the first suffrage petition, but also because it illustrates many aspects of what was causing women to feel such anger and frustration in the mid-nineteenth century. Although her priority was women's medicine, Elizabeth always supported the suffrage movement and her daughter Louisa became a prominent suffragette in the militant campaigns of the early 1900s.

Elizabeth is the most famous of the Garrett sisters but she was not the only one to play a significant role in the suffrage campaign. Her elder sister, Louisa (1835–1867), worked with the others on the Petition. She died only a year afterwards. Agnes (1845–1935) was also an active speaker and campaigner in the cause of suffrage. In 1875 she and her cousin, Rhoda Garrett (who spoke at an Ipswich suffrage meeting in 1871), set up the first all-woman design and decoration company. They did the interior design for the houses of their family and many of the independent women they associated with, also for Elizabeth's hospital for women. The contribution of the second youngest sister, Millicent, is considered later.

---

[*] After Elizabeth Garrett succeeded in becoming a doctor via the Society of Apothecaries, it changed its rules so other women could not achieve the same.

professional standard to that role. A married woman had only just gained the right to keep her property, earnings, inheritance and even her children (though only until they were 7 years old) if she was separated from her husband. There were virtually no rights or protections for working-class women, and double standards as regards sexuality were rife. Some women were beginning to feel that if they had the vote, they might be able to redress some of these issues.

Encouraged by a speech in the House of Commons, on 27 April 1866, by Conservative minister Benjamin Disraeli, in which he said that women should have the right to vote[*], new Liberal MP John Stuart Mill agreed to present a petition to parliament if a hundred signatures could be found. A small working-group was set up which included Louisa and Elizabeth Garrett, Emily Davies and Barbara Bodichon. The group called itself the Women's Suffrage Committee and met in Elizabeth Garrett's London drawing room. Within two weeks, 1,499 women from all over the country had put their name to a petition for the Extension of the Elective Franchise to All Householders without Distinction of Sex.

Of the 1,499 signatories, almost half came from London, Manchester and Leeds. Forty-eight were Suffolk women, of whom sixteen were living in and around Ipswich. It is interesting to note that there were four signatories in Essex, none in Norfolk or Huntingdonshire and one in Cambridgeshire. This is not necessarily because Suffolk had more highly politicised women than neighbouring counties. Rather, as Ann Dingsdale points out in her study of the Petition, it reflects where the networks of the petition's initiators happened to stretch.[3] In addition, some women may have wanted to sign, but were unable to do so. A woman from Kent wrote:

> I doubt if I ever knew a woman who dared do so much as sign a petition without the approbation of the man, husband or other, who determined the amount of cash in her purse and whose temper governed her.[4]

The high number of Suffolk signatories is no doubt due to the fact that Elizabeth Garrett and her older sister Louisa were two of the instigators of the petition. Although they were living in London at the time, clearly they persuaded their family and friends at home to sign. Nineteen women from Aldeburgh signed

---

[*] Despite making this speech, quoted in J. Marlow, *Votes for Women* (2001), Disraeli did nothing to further the cause of women's suffrage either as an MP or as prime minister.

the petition, including several from the Garrett family. This is an extraordinary number for a tiny town. Although it is now famous for its musicians, artists and intellectuals, in the middle of the nineteenth century Aldeburgh was deeply rural and conservative. In fact, after nineteen of its female inhabitants signed the petition, there seems to have been no further suffrage activity in the town for about forty years. Other members of the Kensington Society also had links to women in the Ipswich area.

## The Ipswich women who signed

Along with the sixteen women from Ipswich that signed the petition, three were from Westerfield. About half of the signatories lived in Fonnereau Road and nearby Berners Street. These were some of the streets of Ipswich where the upper and middle classes lived at that time, and one can imagine such women taking the petition to their friends to sign. Several of the women who signed were single women and widows who were heads of their own households, yet had no say in the government of the country. There appear to be no signatories from the neighbouring towns of Hadleigh, Stowmarket, Felixstowe, or Woodbridge, though there might well have been interested women in those places if they had known about it.

Information given here about the women who signed has been gained from a study of the Petition itself;[5] from census records (the Petition was signed halfway between the census of 1861 and that of 1871, making it more difficult to locate women who may have moved during that period); from Ipswich street directories; and from studies by Ann Dingsdale[6] and suffrage historian Elizabeth Crawford.[7] Such records reveal a little about the domestic situation of the signatories, but in most cases we do not know what led them to be sympathetic towards the Petition.

**MARIA ANN ALEXANDER** was about 53 years old when she signed the Petition. She lived at No. 16 Museum Street, Ipswich, with her husband, a wool, wine and spirit merchant, and their three children. This was a big, three-storey Georgian house, which probably included the business premises, very near to the town centre.

**ELIZABETH BARKER** was a widow aged 68 at the time of the Petition, living at No. 30 Berners Street, Ipswich, with a servant. She was the head of the household. Berners Street was built in the 1830s to create a way from the main street to the hospital at the top of the hill. Number 30 no longer exists, but if it was similar to its neighbour, it would have been a detached, double-fronted two-storey house.

**ELIZABETH BOWMAN** also lived in Berners Street, at No. 76, a smaller though still substantial semi-detached two-storey house. She was aged about 50 at the time of the Petition. The 1861 census indicates that she lived with her husband, a musician. However, the street directory of 1864 indicates that she lived alone at this address, so she may have been a widow by the time of the Petition.[8]

**MARIA BURROWS** lived at No. 51 Fonnereau Road, Ipswich – a large double-fronted two-storey detached house. The 1861 census indicates that she was about 80 years old, and was probably the oldest of all the petitioners. She was the head of the household, the widow of a plumber, and lived with a companion and two servants. At that time Fonnereau Road was little more than a footpath with hawthorn hedges on each side leading to the grounds of Christchurch Mansion (now the town's main park).

**ELIZABETH BUTLER** lived at Anglesea House, No. 90 Berners Street (misread in the petition transcript as Bowen St). This a very large house, now largely refurbished and turned into flats, right at the top of the street. Local directories confirm that it was 'an establishment for young ladies' or a 'ladies' school'.[9] The 1871 census shows that Miss Butler, aged 45, was the headmistress, and her younger sister was a schoolmistress. Three teachers were listed, and three servants. Such schools were extremely common for daughters of middle-class families, and there were more than twenty boarding pupils, aged 8–17. As women had no access to higher education, the teachers had little formal education themselves. According to Ann Dingsdale's research, Miss Butler had signed a petition in 1864 to Cambridge University demanding that women be allowed to sit the University Local Exams. She is likely to have been a friend or colleague of Emily Davies, one of the Petition's instigators, who was agitating for these reforms.

**SOPHIA DOUGHTY** lived at No. 13 Westgate Street, which is one of the main streets of Ipswich. At that time it was lined with hotels and shops with living accommodation above, and also had a public hall and a theatre.

**PEGGY GARRETT** also lived in Fonnereau Road, at No. 47, another large house in this road. In Kelly's Directory of 1864, she is listed as living here alone.

**LUCY GOSS** lived at the town end of Fonnereau Road, at No. 9, which is a three-storey terraced town house. The 1871 census gives her age as 53, and states that she is the unmarried head of the household, an 'annuitant', with a lodger and a general servant. Earlier census returns indicate that she ran a dressmaking business.

**JANE COBBOLD SIMPSON** lived at No. 57 Berners Street, and was about 40 when she signed the Petition. The 1871 census identified her as living with her husband Josiah Simpson, a professor of music, and two young children.

**ANN WILSON** of No. 8 Fonnereau Road is said, in the 1861 census, to be aged 55 and living with her husband Henry R. Wilson, house and land proprietor. This is an extremely large house right on the border of Christchurch Park, which was at that time the grounds of the mansion in which the Fonnereau family lived.

No additional information about signatories Susan Appleton, Esther Purvis (Berners Street) and Mary Anne Simpson (St Matthews Street) has been found.

Three women from nearby Westerfield village also signed the petition. The 1871 census says that the village, which is just a couple of miles north-west of Ipswich, had a population of about 314 people in seventy-two houses.

**SARAH BIRD** only gives her address as Westerfield. It is likely that she was the wife of William Bird. The Bird family had lived in Westerfield since the early part of the nineteenth century – at The Manor, a substantial farm with a sixteenth-century timber-framed house – and would continue to do so for several generations. Sarah (1826–1911) would have been about 40 years old when she signed the Petition. According to the 1861 census, William and Sarah had three sons and two daughters aged between 1 and 12. One of Sarah's granddaughters, Edna Hyacinth Bird, was born in 1894, and Hyde and Perkins, in their study of Westerfield say of her: 'In her early days she was a suffragette. She was a teacher ... and moved to Wisbech on her marriage.'[10]

**MATILDA BETHAM EDWARDS** (1836–1919) gives no address alongside her signature on the Petition. She lived in Westerfield until the mid-1860s, and it is possible that she no longer lived in the village at the time of the Petition. She was born at Westerfield Hall and was the fifth child of farmer Edward Edwards and Barbara Betham. She attended the local Westerfield school, but left on her mother's death when she was 10 years old. She educated herself via voracious book-reading, also spending a lot of time with her extended family in London. She desperately wanted a career, and became a pupil-teacher in Peckham. She hated this life, however, and returned home to Westerfield where she wrote and had published her first novel, *The White House by the Sea*, a romance that was very popular and in print for a long time. She wrote many other novels and travelled widely in Europe and North Africa. In 1864, her father died, and she returned to Westerfield where she kept the farm with her sister. On her sister's death a year later, Matilda moved to London where she met Barbara Bodichon, the leader of the radical group that instigated the Petition. Although she strongly identified with women's issues, she was not active in the cause and preferred to concentrate on her successful writing career.

**HANNAH HOPE SIMPSON** simply gave Westerfield as her address on the Petition, and it has not been possible to find any further details of her.

## The campaign for 'Votes for Women' grows

The Petition was presented to newly elected MP John Stuart Mill on 7 June 1866 by Elizabeth Garrett Anderson and Emily Davies. The story goes that when the two women got to the House of Commons, John Stuart Mill was not there, and they took fright and hid the large, heavy scroll under an apple-seller's stall until he came and received it.[11]

Mill presented the petition to the House of Commons, and it was seconded by Henry Fawcett. The women were delighted to hear that not only had it been heard with attention and respect, but that seventy-three MPs had voted in favour (196 voted against).[12] This was not the overwhelming defeat they had expected, although of course it was not enough and could not initiate change in itself. When the next Reform Act was passed the following year, the principle of enfranchising women was not included. A small group of middle-class and professional men were now enabled to vote, bringing the franchise to about 10 per cent of the population – 2.5 million.

Many bleak years followed as regards suffrage for women, but every opportunity was used to further the cause. At the 1868 general election a woman in Manchester, by some chance bureaucratic error, found her name on the electoral register and voted. Some 5,346 other women then applied to the courts for the same liberty. The judges refused, declaring 'every woman personally incapable'.[13] But clearly something was beginning to shift, because in the next year the 1869 Municipal Corporations Act allowed some women (mainly householders) to vote in local council elections. This was followed by legitimising women's activity in relation to the School Boards a year later. Boards were elected, and women could vote and stand as candidates. Elizabeth Garrett Anderson was one of the first women to take up this opportunity. Slowly but surely, it was beginning to be acknowledged that women could and should have influence beyond the domestic sphere.

Campaigns for women's suffrage began to spring up in London and Manchester. These societies, and others beginning to form elsewhere, saw their role as talking to influential people, lobbying, educating, getting the support of MPs and persuading them to take up the cause of women's suffrage in parliament. In fact, there were debates in parliament on women's suffrage in most of the ensuing years of the century, with eventually a majority of MPs stating their support. Private members' bills proposing some enfranchisement of women reached their second readings many times. However, the government was never interested enough to promote them into law.

The third Reform Act of 1884 saw two-thirds of men become enfranchised, including farmworkers, but there was no advance whatsoever in terms of women's right to vote. There began to develop a split in the rapidly growing campaign for votes for women. Societies for Women's Suffrage had so far restricted their demands to votes for women householders – mainly widows and single women. Their argument was that once the principle was accepted that women should have the vote, then would be the time to demand that all women have that right. The limited demand of their campaign was seen as a plea for natural justice by many people who otherwise might not have supported the cause. However, Emmeline Pankhurst and similarly minded women were becoming more prominent in the movement and had formed the Women's Franchise League in Manchester. They insisted that future campaigns must include the vote for all women, and they did not therefore support some of the private members' bills that came before parliament. These and other differences eventually became so strong that, in 1903, the movement split into two.

Despite these arguments, campaigning continued. Further progress was made in 1894 when some married women got the right to vote in municipal elections. This acknowledged for the first time that men were not the only voice of the household. By the end of the century women were gaining more freedoms and powers in relation to education, employment, local politics and influence, and had greater economic status within marriage. However, as regards the ability to vote or be a candidate in a national election, there was no gain, nor any likelihood of imminent change. The reason for this was the prevailing attitude about women's inferior ability to take part in public life, but the politics are also revealing. If women were to get the vote, it could significantly change the political balance. Suffrage writer Diane Atkinson explains this:

> Most [MPs] wanted women to have the vote only if their party benefited: Conservative MPs ... feared that if women were enfranchised they would vote for the Liberals or for the new Labour Party. The Liberals in general believed that women should have the vote but were also afraid that their opponents would benefit. While many Liberal MPs worked for women's suffrage ... many of its senior Cabinet Ministers were die-hard opponents, and they ensured that no progress was made ... The Labour Party, a new party founded in 1892 to represent the interest of working men, was afraid that unless all adults were given the vote, they would not benefit from any changes to the franchise. If property-owning women got the vote and not working-class women, they argued the Conservative and Liberal parties would gain an important advantage.[14]

**MILLICENT FAWCETT** (*née* Garrett), (1847–1929), was the second youngest of the Aldeburgh Garrett daughters. She was only 12 years old when her sister Elizabeth moved to London hoping to find a way of becoming a doctor, and Millicent frequently went to stay with her and her eldest sister, Louisa. Millicent was 18 when she heard a speech by John Stuart Mill, and she became one of his supporters. She also got to know the radical MP for Brighton, Henry Fawcett and, despite him being fourteen years older than her, she married him in 1867. He was a wholehearted supporter of women's suffrage. Her daughter, Philippa, was born a year later. Millicent spent much of her time helping her husband, who was blind, and also wrote books and articles on politics. She was a member of the London Suffrage Committee, and this work increased after Henry Fawcett died in 1884. She became president of the newly formed National Union of Women's Suffrage Societies (NUWSS) in 1897, which sought to bring many disparate local branches under a single leadership and set of policies. She believed in constitutional methods to gain the vote for women, and there were many disputes with more militant suffragists like Emmeline Pankhurst and her daughters, who broke away to form the Women's Social and Political Union (WSPU) in 1903. Although Millicent disagreed with the methods of the WSPU she never openly criticised them and was happy to work with them whenever there were areas of agreement.

At the end of the century, the suffrage campaign was still too tiny to challenge such entrenched attitudes. However, it had begun to bring together all the separate suffrage societies with their different names under one national organisation, of which Millicent Fawcett became president.

## The start of the Ipswich campaign

There was a spate of larger petitions in ensuing years, demanding the vote. Two petitions were presented to parliament by Ipswich women in 1869 and by those in Bury St Edmunds in 1869 and 1871, for example. But there do not seem to have been any local women's suffrage organisations at this time.

Nonetheless, suffrage meetings began to take place, with national speakers coming to the area to lecture and educate, in the hope of encouraging women to set up local branches of the National Women's Suffrage Society. For example, Lydia Becker, Laura Ormiston Chant and other national suffragists came to speak in Bury on several occasions over the next twenty years, and some of the Aldeburgh Garrett family held a meeting at Framlingham in 1871 (where five women had signed The Ladies' Petition). There were meetings in Sudbury in 1883 and 1893. Newspaper reports of these meetings show how timid the demand for the vote still was at this time.

On 21 February 1870, a Miss Couperthwaite came to Ipswich and gave a talk at the Lecture Hall in Tower Street entitled 'A Woman's Views on the Woman's Question'.[15] She argued that in history there are many examples of noble-minded women in public life, and England had been served well by its queens – so why should women not have the vote? She pointed out that 3.5 million women in the country earned their own living and paid taxes. She asked the audience to sign a petition, which Jacob Bright MP had agreed to present, and many did exactly that.

On 12 April 1871 the Lecture Hall was again full of people, women and men, eager to hear about women's suffrage. This meeting was chaired by Edward Grimwade, a leading Liberal in the town, and the speaker was Rhoda Garrett, accompanied by her cousin, Millicent Fawcett. The *Suffolk Chronicle* reported Rhoda's speech in great detail. Her opening remarks were:

Women's suffrage is a subject regarded by many with dislike and fear as a dangerous innovation, or with scorn as the dream of wild enthusiasts, and by most with pitying amusement ...

She went on to list, and then carefully refute, ten reasons commonly put forward as to why there should be no vote for women. This list is worth looking at to see what the arguments were like at this time:

1. It is not natural for women to have the vote.
2. Women have never voted, so why now?
3. Woman's sphere is in the home, and they would neglect their duties if they gave attention to public matters.
4. Women don't want to be enfranchised as their interests are represented by men.
5. Women are too gentle and delicate to be brought into contact with the coarse surroundings of the polling booth.
6. Women are mentally and physically inferior so should be excluded from public life.
7. Men may not still give women fair and courteous attention.
8. If women are allowed to vote, next they would want to sit in Parliament.
9. If the wife had the vote, she might use it in opposition to her husband's wishes.
10. Women are more easily influenced.

Rhoda Garrett dealt with many of these 'reasons' rapidly and humorously. Hidden within this list, however, are the core objections of the time, namely that woman's sphere is the home, and that having the vote might affect the relationship between husband and wife. Millicent Fawcett spoke reassuringly of how the demand for the vote was limited to householders, women who pay taxes and rates – 'that would not subvert the order and tranquillity of domestic life'.[16]

**HARRIET GRIMWADE** (1843–1893) was the daughter of Edward Grimwade, Alderman of Ipswich, mayor, Liberal and Congregational minister. She lived at Norton House, Henley Road, Ipswich. Harriet was engaged in philanthropic work from a young age. She opened a Girls' Home to provide accommodation for young girls coming to Ipswich from the villages around to find work. The home failed, and later she founded Hope House in Foxhall Road, Ipswich, as an orphanage for young girls. There they were educated and trained for domestic service. In 1880, she was the first woman in Ipswich to be publicly elected as a member of the School Board.

The national suffrage newspaper *Women's Suffrage Journal* reported in its July 1871 edition that an Ipswich Committee of the London Society for Women's Suffrage had been formed, and the honorary secretary was Miss Harriet Grimwade of Ipswich. For some reason Harriet did not hold this position for long, being succeeded in 1872 by Mrs Pickford.

The Ipswich Women's Suffrage Society held further meetings occasionally over ensuing years. The focus tended to be on the seemingly uncontroversial proposal, supported by prominent local men, limiting the franchise to women householders. Support was gained by appealing to the natural justice of every household having a vote, no matter who its head was. Despite this, there was no sign of parliament recognising such justice through legislation. Ipswich does not appear to have responded when the campaign for women's suffrage became more militant in 1903, and when Constance Andrews burst onto the town's suffrage scene in 1907, she regarded the society as moribund.

# 2

# STIRRING UP IPSWICH

## Who was Constance Andrews?

Constance Andrews was about 40 years old when she started to work for the vote for women. Despite her being an ardent reformer, trade unionist and the most committed and involved of all the suffragettes in and around Ipswich, details about her background, apart from what we can find on census schedules, are hard to find.

She was born in Stowmarket in 1863/64, so was just a baby when the previously mentioned Suffolk women signed the first petition demanding suffrage for women. Her father was Oliver Andrews, an architect and surveyor, and her mother, Mary, appears to have had no paid occupation as was common with married women at that time. Constance Emily was the middle of three daughters – Mary was one year older, and Lilla three years younger. There was also a little brother, Joseph, seven years younger than Constance.

The family lived in a house in Tavern Street in Stowmarket, from which Oliver also ran his business. Stowmarket was, as it is now, a small market town, and it had a population of about 4,000 people in the middle of the nineteenth century. Tavern Street is near the town centre, and the street also included the police station and court, the workhouse and, when Constance was a teenager, William Pretty & Sons' corset factory. It also housed several shops, including Footmans Drapers and a jeweller. At the furthest end stood two large houses, the gardens of one of which was used as a park by the townspeople.[1]

There were two schools in Stowmarket at that time – the National School, which was a church school, and the British School, which was probably a private school funded by grants and subscriptions. It is probable that the Andrews children went to one of these schools, which were just a couple of streets away from their home. Education appears to have had an important role in this family, as in the 1881 census, when Constance was 17, she is still listed as a 'scholar' alongside her younger siblings.

Constance's father died in his 50s sometime between the census of 1881 and that of 1891. Constance left the family home and went to live at the home of Thomas Cooke, a professor of singing in Gloucestershire. She worked as a schoolmistress – one of the most limited and poorly paid occupations for women of the time. Her sisters Mary and Lilla still lived at home with their mother (there is no mention of Joseph), and were teachers of music.

By the turn of the century, there is no further mention of her mother in records, and Constance was living at No. 11 Gippeswyk Road in Ipswich. For a few years she had her own place to live, here and then at No. 82 London Road, before moving, by 1907, to live with Lilla, her brother-in-law George Pratt and their family at No. 160 Norwich Rd – a large elegant house with eleven rooms.

## Rousing the women of Ipswich

Constance may have come from a social reforming family, or she may have become interested in such issues later. We know from references in her letters that she was active in the world of social reform in Ipswich before she became committed to women's suffrage. For example, in a letter written in 1907 she talks about having canvassed in support of two Poor Law Guardians the year before, and also refers to her organ-playing at the Social Settlement, an organisation which provided services for the poor and unemployed of the town.[2] She cannot have been unaware of the increasing radicalism of the suffrage campaign nationally, and realised that, even as a householder, no matter how hard she worked she would never have the vote in national politics, be able to influence law, or see any woman become an MP if the existing system remained. As a social reformer she might have felt, as many others did, that if women had the vote much might change for the better. She may also have begun to hear in the national press those more strident voices that were beginning to take direct action to achieve change.

Early in 1907, she became secretary of the Ipswich branch of the London Society for Women's Suffrage. In a letter in February of that year she wrote to the secretary of the main organisation in London, Philippa Strachey:

We think it is time to rouse the women of Ipswich and are organising a large meeting for Friday March 15th. I have written to Millicent Fawcett to ask if she can possibly come and speak for us. I find myself handicapped for funds, the late secretary tells me there is no reserve fund. Can you give us financial help? ... I think it is worth making an effort as I believe we shall do some good propaganda work ...[3]

Constance's letter indicates that the lobbying, campaigning, constitutional suffrage organisation that Harriet Grimwade had started thirty-five years previously had faded. It lacked funds and focus and, perhaps, membership. It was ambitious of Constance to invite Millicent Fawcett, who was by now the president of the non-militant National Union of Women's Suffrage Societies, to her first meeting and it must have been disappointing for the enthusiastic new secretary that she did not come.

Ipswich and perhaps Constance Andrews herself were as yet untouched by the militant new campaign of the Women's Social and Political Union (WSPU), which Emmeline Pankhurst and her daughters Christabel, Sylvia and Adela had formed in Manchester in 1903. Emmeline Pankhurst had been a suffrage supporter for many years, but now she and her daughters saw that all the old ways of trying to get suffrage for women had failed. The endless drawing-room meetings, writing to MPs, public meetings, and deputations to the House of Commons had achieved precisely nothing. Any parliamentary debate seemed to lead only to yet another failed private members' bill. The motto of the new WSPU was 'Deeds not Words'.

In fact, it was eight years since even a private member's bill had been introduced to the House of Commons by the time Emmeline Pankhurst persuaded an MP to do so in May 1905, and this move was met with great enthusiasm by all suffrage supporters. Women flocked to the Houses of Parliament on the day, but those that got into the public gallery were less than satisfied. They were forced to listen to a drawn-out discussion on a previous bill, dealing with lights on carts at night, until, as some MPs had intended, there was no time to debate women's suffrage. The initially excited and hopeful women were now furious and indignant, and Emmeline Pankhurst urged them outside for a protest meeting. Hustled and disbanded by the surprised police, they were at last allowed to hold a rally outside Westminster Abbey. It was the first action of its type; women took the initiative and wrested control of the agenda.

Suffragists of all kinds spent the rest of 1905 lobbying candidates for the coming general election. A Liberal success was expected to end years of Conservative government, and they wanted to persuade the Liberal candidates, should they be elected, to support the granting of suffrage to women.

**CHRISTABEL PANKHURST** and **ANNIE KENNEY** were the first suffragettes to be arrested. Late in 1905, during the election campaign, they went to a Liberal political meeting in Manchester and each asked whether, if elected, a Liberal government would give the vote to women. There was no answer. The two women unfurled their banner and insisted on an answer to their question. They were removed from the hall, and later charged with assaulting the police. On appearing in court, they refused to pay a fine, and were taken to prison. Their behaviour was seen as shocking. It was a deliberate attempt to create publicity for the cause.

The new Liberal government was duly elected in 1906, but the suffragists' hopes were immediately dashed when the February 1907 King's Speech, which laid out the programme of the government for the next session of parliament, made no reference to the enfranchisement of women. Processions, demonstrations and intensive lobbying resulted in Prime Minister Sir Henry Campbell-Bannerman agreeing to see a deputation of women in May, only for him to tell them that he could not commit himself to promoting votes for women.

The rest of the year was characterised by failed deputations to Downing Street, by disrupted political meetings, demonstrations, and the arrests and imprisonment of women whom the *Daily Mail* had scathingly termed 'suffragettes' – a label they were proud to wear.*

We do not know what the reaction in Ipswich was to these events, or whether any women from the area were directly involved in them. There may have been debates and discussions about the issues in the trade unions, for example, or the newly formed Independent Labour Party, just like in political protest today. Were the protesters justified in doing what they did? Was the police response proportionate? Would the government change its view? They may have recognised new elements that had not been seen much in women's campaigns before – the persistence of educated, middle-class women who had an eye for maximum publicity, imagery and the most effective action for that moment, which seemed to include going to prison.

---

* The term 'suffragette' has come to apply to those women taking radical, militant action, and the term 'suffragist' to those opting for the more constitutional route. The women and the press of the time often used the labels more indiscriminately.

Waverers, including women who had been working a long time for suffrage via more traditional channels, may have been reassured by Millicent Fawcett, who as president of the National Union of Women's Suffrage Societies (NUWSS) wrote in a letter to *The Times* on 27 October 1906:

> I take this opportunity of saying that in my opinion, far from injuring the movement, they [the Women's Social and Political Union] have done more during the last twelve months to bring it within the realm of practical politics than we have been able to accomplish in the same number of years.

Inspired by the Women's Social and Political Union (WSPU), the NUWSS began to expand its range of activities, though still within its constitutional limits. In February 1907 it organised a procession through London. Encompassing forty of its societies from across Britain, it was led by their president Millicent Fawcett and her sister Elizabeth Garrett Anderson, now retired from her profession as doctor. It was the first open-air demonstration by non-militants, and aspired to match the WSPU for colour, imagery and publicity. For reasons we can easily imagine, it became known as the 'Mud March'. Nevertheless, it was notable for the fact that women from all classes marched side by side; that women in fact marched who never thought themselves capable of doing so, overcoming some of their conditioned responses in the process. It warranted full-page pictures in the press.

Constance Andrews, keen to regenerate the debate about women's suffrage in Ipswich, decided to use the existing organisation as a foundation for her work. Her first public meeting took place at the public hall in Westgate, Ipswich on 15 March 1907. Millicent Fawcett did not accept the invitation to come and speak, and there were attempts to find someone of note. Eventually, a suffragist called Mrs Stanbury came to address the meeting.

The *Evening Star* was there also, and reported the next day:

> Mr W. Rowley Elliston presided and said the ladies' objective in holding the meeting was to put on record their own feelings and those of women of the town on women's Suffrage ... It hadn't been discussed much at the last election, but since then the debate had been forced to the front ... he didn't approve of it all, but he was totally in favour of the enfranchisement of women.

Mrs Stanbury, in her address, was reported to have discussed the issue of taxation without representation. She described women as 'outlanders in their own land'. She referred to their success at high levels in the professions, and 'the excellent work of women in local government, especially as Poor Law Guardians'. A proposal for equal enfranchisement for women with men was narrowly carried.

It may have been a more difficult meeting than the *Evening Star* suggests, at least for women not used to taking a prominent role, for in her letter of thanks to Mrs Stanbury, Constance said:

> I really do not know how to thank you for coming to our aid in Ipswich and making our meeting such a success. I dare not think what would have been the result of having had a weak speaker at such a meeting, it would certainly have been disastrous to our cause here. As it is, I think we can congratulate ourselves on having a good start.[4]

Constance went on to outline some plans for the summer – drawing-room meetings, garden meetings, trying to interest some of the working women that she knew, canvassing the town. Even so early in her career as a campaigner for votes for women, we get a hint of her frustration and isolation: 'I regret I did not have the chance of having a real talk with you, there were many things I would have liked to ask you,' she wrote in the same letter. She expressed regret at being unable to attend a meeting in London, saying 'it would be so refreshing to be for once in the heart of things'.

Constance's next letter to Philippa Strachey showed her to be full of plans[5], talking of three drawing-room meetings to be held during the summer. She appeared to get some support from the letters she exchanged with Philippa, who must have asked her what the local group was like. Constance writes to her in July 1907:

> I do not wonder that you are a little puzzled about the Women's Suffrage Society and I am writing to explain matters as far as possible. Early in the present year I was asked to become Secretary ... Being very keen on the subject I accepted it with perhaps too little thought and I found the movement here in a very moribund condition; there had been no meeting of any sort for a year ... It occurred to me that a good way to awaken interest in Ipswich on the subject would be to hold a large meeting and we did hold one ... the meeting was a success in every way except the ordinary exception – financially ... This left us with a debt of £6 19s 9d which I had to pay, my committee being less enthusiastic than myself ...[6]

Constance also mentioned that there were fifty-six members of the group:

> Our President is Miss Kennet, Headmistress of Ipswich High School and we have 11 Vice-presidents. You will think this is very rich, but at present I have their names and not their subs. I am however hoping for these to come along later.

In a later letter, Philippa concludes 'it would have been such a pleasure to meet you, and to be able to tell you how much I admire the work you have done since you became Secretary at Ipswich'.[7] Perhaps her admiration relates to Constance's persistence in the face of the ongoing problems with her committee, as so far Ipswich appears to have done little to further the cause.

In September 1907, the WSPU, which at that time had no local organisation in the town, mounted a brief campaign, in which Constance became involved. The national suffrage paper, *The Women's Franchise*, reported:

> The Ipswich and Suffolk newspapers gave an excellent account of Mrs Martel's campaign there ... The Ipswich Observer [*sic*] says: the meeting was wholly conducted by ladies, no mere man was allowed to have a voice in the matter. Miss Constance Andrews, a lady of advanced views in our town was

Constance named the eleven vice-presidents of the Ipswich Women's Suffrage Society, and made her own comments on their character and attributes:

Mrs Cullingham – Daughter of Mr Everett, MP

Mr J.B.Fraser – Liberal (of influence in the town)

Miss Griffin – Conservative. Great on Temperance Question

Mrs Griffiths – Liberal, keen on temperance work

Miss Harrison – Headmistress of Girls' Municipal Secondary School

Mr G.T. Moss – JP. Useful working man. ILP

Mrs G. Pratt*

Miss B. Ridley – Liberal – has sent subscription to you this year

Mr A.F. Vulliamy – Conservative. County Coroner

Miss Flear – Kindergarten Mistress at High School

Mrs Hossack

---

\* This is Lilla, Constance's sister. We do not know if she joined the society at the same time as Constance, or was already a member.

in the chair. She made a capital chairman. Three speakers – Miss Lamb, Mrs Hicks and Mrs Martel, the enfranchised lady of Australia, who fought and won there ...[8]

Constance's October meeting of the newly formed Ipswich and County Women's Suffrage Society took place at St Lawrence's Hall, Ipswich in the middle of the campaign for the municipal election, in which about 2,500 Ipswich householder women were entitled to vote (a limited number of women had been enfranchised to vote in local elections since the end of the previous century). The meeting was specifically targeted at women voters. The *Evening Star* reported that in his opening remarks Mr W.T. Griffiths said that women looked on their vote in these elections as being introductory to getting the parliamentary vote. Currently there were no women councillors, but he hoped there would be soon. Mrs Martel and Constance Andrews both spoke, with Mrs Martel describing her Australian experiences and giving examples of how women having the vote had changed things there.

Constance was involved in both meetings, one under the auspices of the WSPU and the other of the Ipswich and County Women's Suffrage Society, and Mrs Martel spoke at both. Mrs Martel belonged to the WSPU, and was apparently a fine speaker appearing at their meetings throughout the country. It is an example of how women may have belonged to one suffrage organisation, but were perfectly happy to support others. This is particularly interesting as, at that time, a fundamental disagreement existed within the WSPU over the authoritarian leadership of the Pankhursts, which had just resulted in the breakaway Women's Freedom League (WFL) being formed, with Charlotte Despard at its head. The WFL became the third big organisation fighting for votes for women. Despite such differences raging in London, elsewhere suffrage supporters were getting on with the campaign.

Constance Andrews' brief correspondence with the London society tells us a little about her. She was committed and perhaps impetuous – going ahead with plans with little support or financial assurance. She seems to have felt isolated and frustrated in her desire for change. In her support of suffrage she was an activist, and one who often wanted to push things on even where there was little encouragement to do so. Of her committee, only two joined her as active campaigners in future years – Mrs Hossack, and her own sister Lilla Pratt – though several others remained committed constitutional suffragists.

# What to do next?

With no further letters available, we have less information about Constance's activities and the development of the Ipswich campaign during 1908. The cycle of educating themselves and others appears to have continued, and the next public meeting was held in March at the Ipswich Lecture Hall; this time Millicent Fawcett, president of the NUWSS, was there. The *Evening Star* reporter called it:

> The most important meeting held yet in Suffolk in connection with the extension of the parliamentary franchise to women. There was a good audience – half a dozen lads heckled in the gallery ... Mrs Griffiths presided, saying the women's movement has travelled far in recent weeks. There had been a debate and division in House of Commons and especially a speech by Herbert Gladstone in support. Many women had been in and out of prison, and there had been a large meeting at the Albert Hall animated with a spirit of deep purpose ... Millicent Fawcett outlined recent successes including the more favourable attitude of the press and the creation of the Men's Suffrage League, and hoped there would be a strong branch in Ipswich. She picked out for criticism Felix Cobbold MP who said taxation and representation going together was an outmoded concept.[9]

The *Evening Star* added that 'Mr H.H. Stansfield appealed for support for the Men's Suffrage League very eloquently'. The Men's Suffrage League had been formed in 1907 in London by men who wished to support the women and their cause in whatever ways they could. The Stansfields would figure later in local suffrage campaigns, but there is no evidence that a branch of the Men's Suffrage League was formed in Ipswich.

During June 1908, two huge and important processions took place in London. They were both in response to the new prime minister, Herbert Asquith, saying that women needed to show him they wanted the vote. The first was organised by the NUWSS, and a procession of 10–15,000 women made their way from the Embankment in London to the Royal Albert Hall, in 'a scene of extraordinary animation and brilliance'.[10] Seventy-year-old Emily Davies, who had worked throughout her life for equality in higher education for women and had presented that first petition demanding the vote for women in 1866, was at the front with Millicent Fawcett. Provincial societies walked in their own block.

According to Lisa Tickner, in her book considering the imagery used by the suffragettes during their campaign, Mary Lowndes made her 'own East Anglian banner emblazoned at Mrs Fawcett's request with the wolf's head, crown and arrows of St Edmund. The motto *Non angeli sed Angli* is Pope Gregory's comment on the English in a Roman slave-market – Not Angels but Citizens'.[11] Mary Lowndes was a stained-glass designer and artist who founded the Artists' Suffrage League in 1907, and created many colourful and intricate banners, postcards and posters for the suffrage movement.

This included a group from East Anglia carrying a banner with the legend: '*Non angeli sed Angli.*'

There were also blocks of international suffragists, doctors and academics, business women, artists, working women, political societies. The crowd of committed constitutional suffragists from all walks of life, with their bright banners, dresses and flowers made a huge impression.

Only a week later, this was followed by the WSPU's response to Mr Asquith's 'request'. This was billed as the 'Biggest Procession Ever', and the WSPU renamed the day as 'Women's Sunday'. Again groups came from all over country, turning up as requested in purple, green and white, creating a pageant of colour. This was the first time that a march was followed by an open-air event in Hyde Park, and it was estimated that there were 250,000 people there, with speakers on twenty platforms.

Since April, the national suffrage papers had advertised special trains coming to the event from all over the country, including one from Ipswich costing 4s 3d return. We can assume that Constance Andrews and some of the Ipswich suffragists were at one or the other of these events along with a great number of women who had never taken political action before.

There was no response from Prime Minister Asquith.

During 1908, Constance had her own experience of democracy. Robert Ratcliffe, in his study of Ipswich's working-class movement at this time, describes how, at the Board of Guardian's election in 1908, the Independent Labour Party had one seat to defend on the Board. They put up two candidates, of which Constance Andrews of the Tailor's Society was one. It was reported that 'Miss Andrews who polled well was not elected'.[12] She had gone from supporting other candidates in 1907 to becoming one herself, perhaps seeing another way in which she could have influence over the matters that interested and concerned her most. Despite this setback, she remained active in issues affecting poor people. The 1909 report of the Independent Labour Party noted: 'Thanks to Comrade Miss Andrews ... and the Women Workers' Federation for their efforts on behalf of the underfed and not fed schoolchildren of Ipswich.'[13]

In October 1908, Sylvia Pankhurst of the WSPU in London's East End came and addressed a meeting in the town. It was a radical step for the Ipswich and County Women's Suffrage Society who organised the event. Newspaper reports indicate that Sylvia, whose commitment was to working women, was in fact standing in for either her mother, Emmeline Pankhurst, or her sister Christabel who were both in prison at that time. Was Constance beginning to feel that more radical measures were needed for women to get the vote, and that the constitutional methods of the traditional organisations were getting nowhere? Whatever the reason for the invitation, the meeting turned out to be something of a disaster, and the people of Ipswich never really got to hear what Sylvia's message was, or that of her co-speaker, Miss Joachim. The *Evening Star* reports that 'when Sylvia Pankhurst rose, pandemonium rose – there was fighting at the back which was very alarming to the women'.[14] The report goes on to say how the hecklers sang, disrupted, and set off stink bombs:

> Sylvia Pankhurst struggled to speak – she said how determined women were, and talked of the different ways in which men had fought to get the vote. [Addressing the disruption] she talked of how often women had been thrown out of halls for minor interruptions, but it seemed the Ipswich police had no power to prevent this [interruption]. Miss Joachim appealed to the audience to deal with the unruly ones, but no-one did and Sylvia Pankhurst said she felt sorry for Ipswich if no-one would deal with them. Mr Fraser [a committee member] tried to get order, but at the same time said he didn't agree with all of what the women were doing. One person was put out by ushers, but it made little difference. Sylvia Pankhurst had tried to speak for one and a half hours.

However, the national suffrage paper *Votes for Women* had a more positive take on the meeting. Its headline read 'FACING THE MUSIC AT IPSWICH':

> For nearly one and a half hours Miss Sylvia Pankhurst refused to be shouted down ... with very real courage ... She clung to her speech and her argument

and seized every opportunity to her advantage. Neither songs nor bells nor rattles nor sulphurated hydrogen, nor the uproar of frequent fights in progress could turn her from her purpose ... it was Miss P's pluck in facing the music which made for the cause a more favourable impression than anything else could have done. Pluck and patience and Pankhurst.[15]

What did the sixteen members of the Ipswich and County Women's Suffrage Society sitting on the 'charmingly decorated platform' think about this disruption? The heckling was of a different order to anything experienced before. We must give credit to Mr Fraser as seemingly one of the only Ipswich people to try to calm things down, though his remarks were compromising and conciliatory. However, Constance Andrews at least was not put off the cause. She may have felt that, in the face of such opposition, a more radical route was the only one to follow. Perhaps, with her trade union and Social Settlement affiliations, she found in Sylvia Pankhurst something of a role model having seen and heard her social ideals and intense commitment at first hand.

Within six months, Constance Andrews had abandoned the organisation she had worked so hard with over two years, and set up a local branch of the Women's Freedom League.

## 3

# HOPE AND DISAPPOINTMENT

## The Women's Freedom League comes to town

> We have during the last two years developed into a fairly strong body and are now independent. Our members include militants and non-militants and both sections are working harmoniously together.

This report by Constance Andrews in the national suffrage monthly, *The Women's Franchise*, of 4 March 1909 gives us some idea of the local situation. The Ipswich and County Women's Suffrage Society had attracted some more militant members, and Constance was hoping to hold together the disparate views of her group. The 25 March edition of the *Evening Star* reports a public meeting of the society, and in its list of platform members the names of Miss Roe and Miss Cay appear, two women who figured in the more radical activity to come in Ipswich.

In May 1909, a number of events coincided which brought this issue of how radical the Ipswich group wanted to be to the fore. These and other new voices prompted Constance, at a meeting called under the auspices of the Ipswich and County Women's Suffrage Society, to urge people to 'join the League – or both the Leagues', meaning the national Women's Freedom League (WFL) and a new local branch.[1] Thereafter she was identified as the secretary of the Ipswich WFL.* The Ipswich and County Women's Suffrage Society did not fold, but continued with its meetings and lobbying in line with its belief in constitutional reform.

The 28 May 1909 was a day which any local suffragette might treasure; it must have seemed that for once the campaign had arrived in town. The day

---

* Information about the different suffrage organisations is given in Appendix Two.

**DR ELIZABETH KNIGHT** (1870–1933) was a Quaker, born in Kent. She went to the newly built Newnham College in Cambridge to read Classics (although women were not allowed to receive degrees at the time), and trained to be a doctor at the London School of Medicine for Women at the same time as Louisa, the daughter of Elizabeth Garrett Anderson. She joined the WFL at its inception in 1907, and was its treasurer many years later. She was a supporter of the 'No Vote, No Tax' campaign and, with her Ipswich friend Hortense Lane, carried out several acts of tax resistance. She went to prison in 1908 when arrested on a deputation to Downing Street, and again in 1913 for refusing to pay income tax. Although she lived in Hampstead, she spent a lot of time in Suffolk, and supported many of the WFL's local events.

began with the auction of Hortense Lane's goods, which had been seized by bailiffs in lieu of the taxes she refused to pay as part of a suffrage campaign called 'No Vote, No Tax'.

Hortense Lane was in her early 30s, and lived with her new husband Frank at Whitton – then a village on the outskirts of Ipswich. This is the first mention of her in reports of suffrage activity. In her tax-resistant actions, of which there were several in this and later years, she was always accompanied by Dr Elizabeth Knight, a well-known London suffragette who lived in Hampstead, London. Hortense, though born in Ipswich, had spent time in London, and may have become part of the WFL there.

Hortense Lane was one of the earliest tax resisters, and the first in Ipswich. This was not a well-known tactic or campaign in 1909 – the inaugural meeting of the Women's Tax Resistance League did not take place for another six months – though one or two women had already taken this course of action. Hortense refused to pay her Inhabited House Duty of 6s 3d, and for several months the tax collector, Mr King, had been calling on her to try and persuade her to do so. In the light of her continued refusal, warrants were issued and eventually the bailiff came round and confiscated a silver fish knife and fork to the value of the unpaid tax.

In line with the procedure of the day, these goods then went to auction to raise the money required, and, on the morning of 28 May, they were included in auctioneer Mr Raphael's weekly sale at the Wolsey auction rooms in Ipswich. The *Suffolk Chronicle* reports under its headline of 'No Say, No Pay':

Extraordinary scenes were witnessed at Ipswich on Friday morning when there was sold by public auction the property of a voteless suffragette woman who had declined to pay taxes on the grounds that tax and representation should go together. The auction became a Votes for Women meeting. Mr Raphael agreed that Mrs Marion Holmes of the Women's Freedom League could mount the rostrum and address the crowd. She wore a smart green gown, a green hat trimmed with cowslips and a green, white and gold scarf – with a silver badge showing that she'd been in prison. Round her stood Mrs Lane, Constance Andrews of the Ipswich and County Women's Suffrage Society, Mrs Knight, Miss Roe, Mrs G. Pratt, Miss Ada Ridley and Mrs Hutley and other local supporters. Mrs Holmes explained the tax campaign – her earnestness and manner made a deep impression on the crowd which applauded again and again. The fish slice and fork were auctioned for 17s, and given back to Mrs Lane. They had made their protest, and a very effective and dignified protest it was too.[2]

Marion Holmes had come from London in support and was to have a busy day. That afternoon, a garden party was held at the Normans' home at Manningtree. Ellen Constance Norman was in her late 30s at the time, and had just married George Kensit Norman, JP. Ellen Norman came from Australia, a country in which women already had the vote, and though we do not know how long she had been in the UK, this may have informed her views. This garden party was attended by local suffragists and suffrage supporters and, with the help of Marion Holmes' experience and knowledge, there was an open discussion of tactics, and what might work well locally. Constance had come to believe that the Ipswich focus on meetings and lobbying was no longer enough, and now there were new, more radical voices to support her.

The garden party was not the end of the day's excitement. That evening they held an open-air meeting on the Cornhill in Ipswich, at which 500 people turned up. At first Marion Holmes and the other women got a good hearing, but the jeers and hostility of parts of the crowd began to take over, and the police decided the women were at risk and advised them to end the meeting. This would not be the last time that heckling affected their plans. As the day drew to a close, Marion Holmes addressed another meeting, this time at the Social Settlement in Ipswich – a working families' centre where Constance was active.[3]

Perhaps this day, so full of activity and excitement, acted as a kind of watershed for Constance Andrews. She may have felt inspired by new suffragettes wishing for more radical action. She may have felt for once part of the wider movement, and responded to the need for more radical and colourful action. The Women's Freedom League would provide that.

The summer of 1909 saw new campaigning strands nationally which also affected East Anglia. These were designed to take the suffrage message to small villages and towns where it had not been heard before, and to offer support where one or two women were fighting on their own. The WSPU focused on a 'holiday campaign' whereby if suffragettes went on holiday to the coast, they would link up with any local supporters, give open-air talks on the prom or the market square, and hand out leaflets. The suffrage press suggests that there were two successful campaigns in Suffolk, at Lowestoft and Southwold, despite there being no local organisations there.

The WFL continued with the caravan campaign it had started the year before, which came to Suffolk for the first time. Indeed it seems that the local branch had been raising money for this, because Elizabeth Knight reports in *The Women's Franchise* of 5 August that the 'Ipswich branch showed such energy and initiative in collecting money for a second caravan that everyone felt it only just and right that they have it for the first season'. The caravan left Ipswich for Debenham, and Dr Knight continued:

> People had given a gloomy account of the unfriendliness we were likely to meet with from the villagers, but all along the route women waved us encouragement, and on our arrival people took a great deal of trouble finding us a pitch. We are settled in a field by a stream and have invited village women to come and talk this afternoon. The van with the flag gaily floating in the breeze is of great interest to passers by.

It went up to Norwich via Bungay, where Constance Andrews joined it for a while, and then east to the coast and southwards.

Like all suffrage campaigns, this was both liberating and extremely hard work. Photos show what we might call a Romany-type caravan drawn by one or two horses, festooned in suffrage posters and banners. One or two men accompanied the small group of women to see to the horses and offer some protection. Suffrage historian Jill Liddington makes the following comment:

> The rigours of travel demanded practical clothes and permitted new identities. Greatcoats, white shirts and ties suggest that vanning, like women-only colleges at university, created a liberating space. Vanning offered a transforming

experience: hatlessness allowed Edwardian suffragettes to embrace all the masculine freedoms evoked by Rebecca West's open road.[4]

At the same time, travelling, bad weather, looking after themselves, and speaking to crowds who might be welcoming or hostile, could well have been a gruelling experience.

The fight for votes for women, as it showed itself in London, had within it two distinct aspects – the increased use of unlawful activity and the development of the political campaign.

That the government was ignoring the message of the huge marches of the previous summer and the protests of the women became clear in February 1909 when there was no mention in the King's Speech of any parliamentary action to enfranchise women. The WSPU in particular felt that they needed to use more direct action to avoid being continuously brushed off. Stone-throwing and window-breaking became commonplace, and continued disruption at political meetings saw any woman suspected of being a suffragette banned from them. The prime minister and senior ministers had to have police escorts wherever they went – a practice virtually unknown at that time. Women in prison were hunger striking to try and get political prisoner status, and those with longer sentences often had to be released early because of the precarious state of their health.

The political campaign was strengthened by the way in which professional women were contributing their skills to the campaign. The development of the Writers' and Actresses' Franchise Leagues and of the Artists' Atalier led to an enrichment of the campaign through an intertwining of art and politics not seen before. The imagery of the movement became important. For example, in April 1909, the NUWSS organised a Pageant of Women's Trades and Professions which included messages about the situation of middle-class women who wanted to work, and working-class women who had to, often in very poor conditions. Artists of all kinds helped women with the materials to create such a pageant and when the day came round, 1,000 women from ninety jobs and professions (including pit-brow women, glassworkers and secretaries) marched at dusk to the Royal Albert Hall. Each group of women from a trade or profession wore their work clothes and carried emblems representing their work. Thousands more followed behind.

The next month, the WSPU took over the Knightsbridge Skating Rink for a couple of weeks and held an enormous exhibition, which included dancing, the first all-woman drum and fife band, stalls and speeches. Inside and out was decorated in purple, green and white – the intention being that these colours become an instant symbol of woman's demand for the vote. The exhibition was a huge success and large amounts of money were raised for the movement.

Events such as these also enabled women to bring all their skills and accomplishments to the aid of their cause. This included doing things for which there was otherwise no opportunity – for example, at this time women could not play instruments in orchestras, and percussion and wind instruments were particularly frowned upon.

The prime minister, Herbert Asquith, continued to refuse to receive deputations of suffragettes, including two women sent via the Post Office as a human letter.* As a result the WSPU decided to invoke a clause in the 1689 Bill of Rights that allowed citizens the constitutional right to petition the king. Their aim was not to lobby the monarch, however, but to approach, once more, the assembly who they argued were his representative – parliament. In June, Emmeline Pankhurst and several venerated older campaigners led a deputation to Downing Street. The prime minister, however, refused to accept their petition. Emmeline Pankhurst talked in her memoirs of the 'old miserable business of refusing to leave, being forced back by the police, pressing forward again and eventually being arrested' – a reminder of how arduous and unglamorous this work was.[5] In support of this action, women threw stones at the windows of the Home Office and other government buildings. In court, Emmeline Pankhurst had to promise that the WSPU would not take any further action until the High Court ruled as to whether the prime minister had to receive the deputation by law.

In dramatic fashion, the WFL supported their sister organisation by staging a sit-in or 'Great Watch', maintaining a presence at both Downing Street and the House of Commons from July–November 1909, day and night, whenever parliament was in session. One day the vigil would be kept by nurses, the next by university women and so on. The continued presence of women who made such a contribution to society, and yet were voteless, made a considerable impact.

---

* A change in the Post Office regulations permitted the posting and transmission of human letters. In *Unshackled*, Christobel Pankhurst describes an incident where two suffragettes were duly posted as human letters addressed to the prime minister at Downing Street, and were led by a telegraph boy to their destination where acceptance was refused.

Now, however, it was the government's turn to escalate matters. Previously, if women went on hunger strike, they were released as soon as they became dangerously weak. This resulted in some women, who were serving longer sentences for more serious actions, being freed well before the end of their sentence. Now the government ordered that women be forcibly fed if they refused to take food, and this was started in Birmingham's Winson Green prison in September 1909. Here is the testimony of Mary Leigh, one of the first:

> The wardress forced me onto the bed and two doctors came in. While I was held down a nasal tube was inserted. It is two yards long, with a funnel at the end ... The end is put up the right and left nostril on alternative days. The sensation is most painful – the drums of the ears seem to be bursting and there is a horrible pain in the throat and the breast. The tube is pushed down 20 inches. I am on the bed pinned down by wardresses, one doctor holds the funnel end, and the other forces the other end up the nostrils. The one holding the funnel end pours the liquid down – about a pint of milk ...[6]

Her report was smuggled out and published in the suffrage press whilst she was still in prison. Afraid that she might die, the government released her early.

Despite people being shocked and appalled, and doctors making strong protests to parliament, forcible feeding formed the backdrop to suffrage campaigns over the next few years. Women suffered with protracted, grim determination, day after day, and often had to be nursed back to health on their release. Some were also said to suffer long-term damage.[7]

Meanwhile, the new Ipswich WFL continued to try and increase public support and demand for the vote, borrowing ideas from the national campaigns where appropriate.

Towards the end of July 1909, they held a Green, White and Gold Fair, inspired by the WSPU's immense London Exhibition and similar smaller events around the country. With Constance Andrews as organiser, supported by new and old members of the group, they hired the Gainsborough Hall in Bolton Lane, Ipswich for the day. This was an enterprising venture for a small group of women. Campaigners came from London to help and remained in the area for a few days, holding public meetings at Ipswich and Woodbridge.

The walls of the hall were 'covered with cartoons illustrating the aims of the movement, and a banner featuring the entrance to Holloway with the words

"Stone walls do not a prison make". In the morning, a decorated lorry went around the town on which were placed nine little girls representing countries where women already had the vote,[*] with Britannia "sitting forlornly" behind labelled "No Vote for Britannia".[8]

In the hall, the fair was opened by Muriel Matters, a radical London suffragette, and featured stalls both of propaganda and information, and of goods for sale to raise funds. There was a mock-up of a Holloway prison cell, of precisely the same size, where Elizabeth Knight took on the role of one of the prisoners and Lillie Roe that of the wardress.

In addition, Mrs Hossack arranged a 'living waxworks' section. There was, for example, a model wife rocking a cradle with one foot, stirring a saucepan with one hand and holding a half-darned sock in the other; also a policeman hears a woman cry 'Votes for Women' and hurries her off to prison.

The waxworks, which had been devised by Cecily Hamilton of the Actresses' Franchise League, are a good example of how activities were developed not just for the big events in London, but for the use of groups around the country – also of how the artistic skill and imagination of suffragettes was harnessed for the campaign.

The caravan campaign of 1909 in Suffolk was largely carried out by national WFL activists. Perhaps this was because Constance Andrews' attention was taken up by her other responsibilities. At the beginning of September, the Trade Union Congress was being hosted by Ipswich and, as secretary of the local Women's Workers' League, Constance was part of the Local Reception Committee – the only woman amongst eighteen men. This committee organised the congress, making all the arrangements for the 500 delegates, as well as for its social events involving local dignitaries. The congress appears to have been a great success. Clearly, Constance had a high profile in the town, and continued with her trade union work alongside her suffrage campaigning.

The summer ended with a significant expansion of the Ipswich WFL. At the end of August, a branch was formed at Hadleigh by WFL supporter Mrs Bastian, and several successful meetings were held at Felixstowe, though it seemed that no one could be found to form a separate branch. Dr Elizabeth Knight, on her

---

[*] Women had the right to vote in New Zealand, Australia, Finland, Norway and several states in America, including Wyoming, Utah, Idaho, Colorado and Washington.

regular visits to Hortense Lane, brought much of her skills, enthusiasm and support to the campaign, which one can only believe were welcomed whole-heartedly by Constance.

## So near ...

The year 1910 started with great hope but ended in despair as far as the suf-fragettes were concerned. At the general election in January, all the suffrage organisations were active in their own ways, promoting and supporting pro-suffrage candidates whatever party they came from, and campaigning as vigorously as the candidates themselves. The London WSPU, for instance, sent a group to Eye to persuade the Liberal candidate to support suffrage if elected. Such campaigns still had the power to surprise metropolitan suffragettes into slightly patronising comments: 'The difficulty of making the claims of the suf-fragettes understood in an agricultural district with time so short, and some electors unable to read, was great. But the interest of the women was marked.'[9] In Ipswich, Constance Andrews and the WFL kept their suffrage colours vis-ible throughout the campaign, especially during the visit of Prime Minister Asquith to the town.

The Liberal government was returned with a significantly reduced majority. Local candidates of all the political parties had now lost favour amongst some of their female supporters and many suffragettes now refused to work for them if they were not active in favour of the suffrage cause. For example, the Ipswich and County Women's Suffrage Society passed a resolution in December 1909 withdrawing support from the political parties until they enfranchised women – the proposers Miss Flear (Lib.) and Miss Lillie Roe (Con.) were ardent workers for their local parties, which would be hurt by that withdrawal.[10]

A period of truce was declared by the suffrage organisations so the new government could consider its position on giving the vote to women. A Conciliation Committee was formed of MPs of all parties to debate the issue. The suffragettes had high hopes, especially as the chair of the committee was the supportive Lord Lytton, whose delicate sister, Constance Lytton, was a fore-most suffragette. Under discussion was a bill that would enfranchise a small number of wealthy women and independent householders. Many suffragettes were deeply opposed to such a limited bill, but hoped that if the principal of women voting were established, it could be rapidly extended to other women.

❖

**GRACE ROE** (1885–1979) was born in London to parents who were interested in suffrage and socialism. She joined the WSPU in 1908, immediately becoming an organiser, and came to Ipswich in 1909 where she lived at No. 19 Silent Street. It was said that there was only one member of WSPU in Ipswich when she arrived. In 1913, as the leaders of the WSPU increasingly found themselves in prison, she returned to London to co-ordinate the national campaign. She was arrested many times, and was apparently forcibly fed 167 times, suffering permanent damage to her throat and digestive system. Later in life, she lived with Christabel Pankhurst in America, where she worked as a social worker.

The organisations had little to do but try to consolidate their networks across the country and focus on lobbying and public education. In this spirit, Grace Roe came to Ipswich to organise the WSPU campaign in Suffolk, applying her energy and London-based networks to great effect.

The WSPU focused a lot of energy on getting the support of more middle-class, richer women, and several drawing-room meetings took place. An innovation was the establishment of a WSPU shop, first at their office at No. 4a Princes Street, Ipswich, then at No. 2 Dial Lane, and later in Tower Street. The shop window was decorated in purple, green and white and displayed posters and the latest edition of their magazine, *Votes for Women*. Inside, people could buy propaganda books, suffragette games, sashes and scarves, and there were also fund-raising items. For many years, Evelyn King co-ordinated the running of this shop.

On 6 May 1910, Christabel Pankhurst, by then the most prominent of the Pankhurst daughters in the campaign, spoke at the Ipswich Corn Exchange to an audience of over 1,000 people. The reporter of the *East Anglian Daily Times* went to London the day before to interview her, and reminded her of the noisy, disruptive meeting her sister, Sylvia, had presided over the year before. Christabel said she did not expect this to happen again (and indeed it did not). She particularly pointed out to the reporter how ludicrous it was that Elizabeth Garrett Anderson, who was now retired as England's first female doctor, and had recently held the position of Mayor of Aldeburgh, still did not have the vote. The meeting was a resounding success. According to the reporter, the stage was beautifully decorated with purple and white flowers, and 'the most expensive seats were taken by the professional men of the town with their wives'. Many working women were there and a great number appeared in their uniforms. Apparently Christabel talked for an hour with no notes, giving a 'clever and persuasive' speech.[11]

The WFL had also become strong enough to hire their own premises by now – at No. 15 Friars Street, which they called their 'club house'. It was here that they continued to meet, sometimes having speakers from the London WFL, sometimes arranging local campaigns and educating themselves (for example, they held sessions on building confidence in public speaking, dealing with hecklers and so on). They also had an innovative way of publicising themselves – a barrow which they placed on the Cornhill. They decorated it with banners and propaganda, and sold items to raise funds.

Reports of local activities in their respective suffrage newspapers suggest that the local WFL and the new WSPU worked separately along their own lines during this year. There is a hint of a slightly tense relationship between the two organisations. One of the main propaganda tools of each was their national weekly newspaper – *Votes for Women* for the WSPU, and *The Vote* for the WFL. These papers, both fairly recently formed, were the first newspapers run by women for women. They reported on their different campaigns, and were also highly educational in terms of how politics works, the history of famous women and their position in society. They also carried cartoons, humorous pieces, short stories and poetry. Designed to be inspirational and forward-looking, the papers carried key messages and information about the cause. Selling them became the focus of a large amount of energy and time for both organisations.

Before the WSPU came to Ipswich, Constance Andrews' WFL had been selling its paper in the market – an obvious place to sell because of the large numbers of women coming and going. At the end of May 1910, Constance reported that their successful sellers of *The Vote* had been banned from the marketplace. 'Another suffragette magazine asked permission to sell,' she wrote, 'and they couldn't have two, so now there are none.'[12] This is how Grace Roe describes the incident: 'Owing to the great interest aroused, it has been decided to sell *Votes for Women* outside the market place next Saturday, as the Town Clerk fears obstruction.'[13]

The usual summer demonstrations in London were postponed for a few weeks because of the death of King Edward VII in May. These were designed to support the process of the Conciliation Bill, of which the suffragettes had come to have high hopes. The June procession was said to be 2 miles long – by far the biggest yet. The *East Anglian Daily Times* reporter was impressed: 'What could be more beautiful and more simple than the hundreds of tiny pennons in the League's colours embroidered with its initials?' He goes on to name sixteen members of the Ipswich WFL who were there. Of the WSPU the reporter says: 'The Ipswich women walked under a banner of purple silk and velvet designed and made by Miss Ada Ridley, with the motto Be Just and Fear Not.' He names twenty-one women from in and around Ipswich walking with the WSPU.[14] This was a strong contingent from Ipswich (there may have been others with other groups), and it also shows how successful the WSPU had been in recruiting women in the few months it had been active in the town.

In June the Women's Franchise (Conciliation) Bill, agreed by all committee members, was introduced into the House of Commons to great acclaim, and two days in July were set aside for its second reading. When Emmeline Pankhurst came to Ipswich to speak on 18 July 1910, hopes were high. Again, a large crowd gathered at the public hall and heard 'her deep and inspiring voice and manner'.[15] However, on 23 July, the day of another large London procession in support of the bill, Prime Minister Herbert Asquith announced that the Conciliation Bill would not be allowed any further parliamentary time that session. The women were bitterly disappointed, and despaired of the political process. The truce held, however, while they considered tactics.

Locally, the education campaign continued. The WFL's caravan was out again during the summer, mainly in Felixstowe. On this occasion, Constance Andrews reported good support from the WSPU as well as from national members on holiday there (three of the five people in the picture are not local – *See* image No. 5).

An example of successful co-operation was the joint lobbying of Ipswich MP Sylvester Horne of the Liberal party, who in November received a deputation of members from the local WFL, WSPU, Ipswich and County Women's Suffrage Society and two other organisations. He agreed at this meeting to continue to press the prime minister to allow time for the Conciliation Bill.

The WFL must also have been busy with its preparations to bring the Pageant of Great Women to Ipswich in October. The pageant had been written by Cecily Hamilton of the Actresses' Franchise League (AFL) (who had also devised the waxworks used by Ipswich suffragettes at the Gold, White and Green Fair the year before) and it was first produced at the Scala in London, in 1909. The project had been suggested by Edith Craig (daughter of the great Shakespearean actress and AFL President Ellen Terry) as a way of involving large numbers of suffragettes in artistic propaganda with a minimum of professional support. Over the next year it was produced in many towns across Britain, using local suffragettes as actors. The pageant was a collaboration between the AFL and the Women Writers' Suffrage League, two groups whose purpose was to put art to the aid of the suffragette organisations' political purpose. Other similar organisations were the Artists' Suffrage League, who helped design and choreograph the enormous processions, and helped women create attractive banners, posters and so on; and the Musicians' League who contributed songs and instrumentalists to meetings and processions.

The pageant presented a theme which revolved around how male prejudice prevents women from fulfilling their potential. In the first scene Justice sits on her throne, and Woman enters pursued by Prejudice, who says she can only live in the shadow of man. Woman refutes this. Then various groups of women enter (Learned Women, Artists, Saintly and Heroic Women, Rulers and Warriors), each with a couple of lines about how successful women are and have been. Prejudice slinks away and Justice declares Woman free.

The event was staged on 20 October 1910 in Ipswich, hosted by Constance Andrews and the Ipswich WFL. Constance's brother-in-law, George Pratt, organist and music teacher, opened with an organ recital and there were girls dancing as well. Charlotte Despard, national leader of the WFL, came to support the occasion, and spoke of how the pageant reminds us of how great women can be. The play was directed by Edith Craig, and Cecily Hamilton played Justice with other national suffrage actors playing Prejudice and Woman. About twenty local women played the remaining parts.

**CHARLOTTE DESPARD** (1844–1939) was radical from a young age. She was devastated by the death of her husband in 1890, and for several years worked with the poor. She became interested in suffrage, and joined the Pankhursts' Women's Social and Political Union. However, in 1907, she and others became unhappy with the authoritarian nature of the WSPU leadership, and broke away to form the Women's Freedom League. It was a less militant organisation than the WSPU, but still radical. Charlotte Despard came to Ipswich many times to speak, and to support the local WFL branch here. Constance Andrews became a close colleague, perhaps a friend, and the two women sometimes campaigned together.

The play would have had an impact on an audience used to this kind of entertainment, though not with this precise focus. It was also an opportunity for the women to dress up in gorgeous clothes, deliver their lines in a dramatic way and presumably have a great time while promoting an important message.

A successful, hopeful, and relatively peaceful year of campaigning came to a dramatic end, with the enfranchisement of women little nearer than it had been forty years earlier. By November, it seemed likely that parliament would be dissolved, meaning that the Conciliation Bill would fall and have to be started from scratch again if the government did not support it. On 18 November, the WSPU brought together hundreds of suffragettes from all over the country at Caxton Hall in London. Small groups of very distinguished suffragette women, some elderly, including Elizabeth Garrett Anderson, left to go to Downing Street, followed in small parties by others. The first women were allowed through and cordoned off, though as usual no senior government minister would meet with them. Those behind, however, were not treated so courteously. Rather than protecting the women, the many policemen in the crowded street appeared unable, or unwilling, to prevent irate men from abusing and assaulting them. It was the women, however, that got arrested, 170 of them in total (including Ipswich WSPU organiser Grace Roe). In a possible attempt to sidestep criticism of the police actions, all were discharged unless they had engaged in violence. Evidence taken later by the suffrage organisations from the women involved showed that several sexual assaults had taken place, either by men in the crowd or possibly by police themselves. Two suffragettes died after this event, said to be because of police brutality, and the day became known as Black Friday.

Lord Lytton and more constitutionally minded suffragists were furious with the WSPU – they felt this action had jeopardised what he was still hoping to achieve with the prime minister regarding the Conciliation Bill. In fact, the country was soon thrown into another general election. Everything would have to start all over again.

# 4

# 'NO VOTE, NO CENSUS'

## If women don't count, don't count women

A new Liberal government was re-elected early in 1911, and the suffrage organisations resumed their truce whilst a new Conciliation Bill was brought forward. All Prime Minister Asquith had to do was to agree to give it parliamentary time in the King's Speech on 5 February. At its AGM on 30 January, the Women's Freedom League (WFL) decided that if he did not do so, they would boycott the upcoming census. If women did not count, they decided, they would not be counted.

The ten-year census was due to be taken on 2 April 1911. Ideas for a campaign related to the census had been under consideration for several months. The WFL was developing at this time a belief in the power of passive resistance, and had determined that until women were given the vote, they should cease business with the government. Its sister organisation, the Women's Tax Resistance League (WTRL), developed much of the detail about the census action. The WTRL had been campaigning for a couple of years on tax resistance, on the basis that although equal taxes were demanded from women, unlike men they had no say in how those taxes were spent. To the WTRL, the requirement to complete the census seemed to fall into the same bracket. Women should not be asked to give information about themselves, if they had no say in how that information was to be used.

The census has always been an important feature of British life. Since 1801 the population has been counted every ten years – although until 1911 only a few basic facts were collected – and the information used to inform policy and spending. Even today, when government departments have so much information about us on its databases and computer systems, the census is seen as important. It has always been, and still is, an offence to refuse to complete the census schedule.

The 1911 census was seen as particularly important. The Liberals had been in power for about five years after a long period of Conservative government, and they were looking for radical reform. They had already brought in such significant measures as the start of Old Age Pensions and the National Insurance scheme. Having won both general elections of 1910, they were anxious to press on with other reforms to improve the housing, health and welfare of the poorer members of the community. John Burns of the Local Government Board was the minister in charge of the census – he was the first working-class cabinet member and one of a large family – and he added in some further questions to the basic information that had been required previously. These questions required the householder to state how many children had been born in the present marriage, the total born alive, and of these, how many were still living and how many had died. With this extra information the government hoped to do something about child mortality.

The new questions were seen by some as a gross intrusion into peoples' private affairs. In addition, the government seemed to have no idea that to ask the head of the household to answer such personal questions relating to what was traditionally woman's domestic sphere, might seem offensive to women who had no say in how the information might be used.

The census boycott began to be talked about in the national suffrage press from mid-February 1911, and although it had been initiated by the WFL, the Women's Social and Political Union (WSPU) decided to support it. In a rare pooling of resources, the two organisations worked together on the development of the ideas, with the WTRL providing legal advice on various options and their possible consequences. The newspapers, *The Vote* and *Votes for Women*, carried weekly 'Question and Answer' pages in which they tried to consider every eventuality, and offer facts and reassurance to women. Local branches began to debate the issues and arrange public meetings to explain the action and get wider support for it.

The best way of conducting the census boycott evolved over ensuing weeks, under the general principle and slogan: 'If women don't count, don't count women'. Two distinct types of action emerged. The first of these was census resistance. This involved a householder refusing to complete the census schedule, and writing across it the reasons why – for example, 'NO VOTE, NO CENSUS'. Refusing to complete the schedule was an offence, and there was the possibility of a £5 fine if a prosecution followed. If no fine was paid, a seven-day prison sentence could be imposed.

The second type of action was census evasion, and this was not illegal. Women were at no risk of prosecution if they were away from home on the night of the census: Sunday, 2 April 1911. It was acknowledged that there were suffrage supporters who, for many reasons, would not risk fines or imprisonment, perhaps because of work or childcare responsibilities, or because they did not feel it right to commit an act of civil disobedience. However, by not being at home to complete the census form, the aim of depriving the government of the information it needed would be accomplished, but without the risk of prosecution. In her absence, the householder would not be able to fill in her details on the schedule.

Suggestions for how women could evade included travelling all night, being at social gatherings in public halls throughout the night, or staying in someone's house where the householder was prepared to say he/she did not know the names of who was staying there.

The census boycott had many advocates in political and artistic circles. One of these was Laurence Housman, a long-term supporter of women's suffrage, who in the weeks before census night embarked on a tour of Britain, including Bury St Edmunds and Ipswich, to explain and get support for the action.

In his columns in *The Vote* in the lead-up to census night, Laurence Housman articulated the feelings of many – that women were going to prison and becoming ill with hunger striking and the subsequent brutality of forcible feeding, but the government just went about its business as usual. Boycotting the census should, for once, harm the state more than the protester, and this was the main beauty of the action. Unlike tax resistance, it also had the advantage that it would take place countrywide on a single night, and women could support each other in taking action.

**LAURENCE HOUSMAN** (1865–1959) was a writer and illustrator, and lived with his suffragette sister Clemence in London. He was a strong supporter of women's suffrage, and a founder member of the Men's Franchise League. He wrote several suffrage plays – including a sketch called *Women This and Women That*, which was often performed at suffrage meetings. He was particularly interested in tax resistance and the census action because he felt strongly that most of the suffragettes' actions harmed themselves more than the state.

When the King's Speech, on 5 February 1911, neither made reference to women's suffrage, nor committed parliamentary time to the passage of the Conciliation Bill into law, Housman said in *The Vote* that any government which refused to recognise women must be met by women's refusal to recognise the government. 'Do we believe in helping the government gather facts and figures which will be used for making laws to govern women without their consent?'[1] This question went to the very heart of democracy.

## Census boycott controversy

Despite the confidence of the Women's Freedom League (WFL) and the Women's Social and Political Union (WSPU), the census boycott was far more controversial within the suffrage societies than might be expected. Suffrage historians Jill Liddington and Elizabeth Crawford describe this conflict as 'welfarism versus suffragism'.[2] On the one side of the conflict were those who wanted the government to have better information in order to make welfare reforms on issues that were of great relevance to women. They wanted to ensure the accuracy of that information, even if they found the questions intrusive. The counterargument was that these were intimate questions relating to women as mothers, and that women should refuse to assist a government that denies them citizenship. Moreover, it was not simply a matter of making a personal choice – for the campaign to succeed, there had to be mass resistance or evasion, and bold, eye-catching actions with their attendant publicity.

It did not help that the largest suffrage organisation, the National Union of Women's Suffrage Societies (NUWSS) decided not to join in. This must have been a huge disappointment to the suffragettes, as they had hoped that this was a campaign that the constitutional, non-militant, more conservative suffragists of the NUWSS could support. Census evasion did not involve breaking the law and, given the continued failure over decades to bring about women's suffrage by constitutional means, was a campaign which all suffrage supporters might feel able to take part in. At this time, the NUWSS had a massive 20,000-plus membership, with branches in towns and villages across the country and its support of the boycott would have made a real impact.

However, this was not to be. At its AGM in January 1911, the NUWSS decided not to support the census action. It resisted ferociously all attempts by the WFL and the WSPU to persuade it otherwise. On 21 March, Philippa Strachey, the secretary of the powerful London Society for Women's Suffrage, wrote to the editors of all the national newspapers to make its position clear. Her letter was published in *The Times* on 23 March 1911:

> As there appears to be a disposition in the press to regard all women suffragists as committed to the policy of refusing to fill up census papers, I am instructed to inform you that a Resolution in opposition to this cause has been passed unanimously by the Executive committee.

Whilst the main suffragette papers remained enthusiastic and positive about their campaign, the national newspapers reflected the battle for hearts and minds that was going on. Professor Michael Sadler of Manchester University used the letter pages of *The Times* to label the census boycott as a 'crime against science' in depriving the government of the information it needed to bring forward legislation to improve the lives of people.[3]

People began to line up for and against, taking moral and political positions – the radical suffragettes on one hand; some of the Liberal intelligentsia, scientists, politicians, constitutional suffragists, the Women's Co-operative Guild and many other organisations on the other. *The Times*, in its leader of 31 March 1911, urged women not to take part saying that 'the logic of it would be ludicrous if it were not too serious to laugh at'; and berated 'those who think to gain the suffrage by showing that they do not deserve it ...' But just in case anyone should think *The Times* was taking it seriously, it ended with a rather offensive 'common sense will prevail'.

*The Manchester Guardian*, the most liberal of the newspapers, carried many articles reflecting both sides of the arguments, but its leader on 1 April 1911 also urged women not to resist or evade. It underlined its commitment to women's suffrage, but asked women to regard the census as merely an information-gathering tool to inform social policy, with rights or reform having nothing to do with it.

In Ipswich, and presumably elsewhere also, the local councils urged the government to make time for the Conciliation Bill and give even a small number of women the vote. They argued that this would allow such moral dilemmas to be taken out of political life and make these kinds of problematic actions redundant.[4]

## Preparations in Ipswich

Constance Andrews, as secretary of the Ipswich branch of the WFL, was central to local preparations for the census action. It was a busy time for her. She was already planning the move of the WFL offices from No. 13 Friars Street to larger premises at No. 16 Arcade Street. This move took place in March, and was followed by a 'hard-up' party, indicating that funds were limited. In addition, she had decided to increase her own commitment to the cause of women's suffrage by not paying for a new dog licence, on 1 January 1911, as part of the Tax Resistance campaign, knowing that there would be consequences of such an action.

The national WFL weekly paper *The Vote* reported on 18 February that, at their recent meeting, the Ipswich branch had considered the fact that no time had been allowed in the King's Speech on 6 February for the Conciliation Bill, and 'a good audience gathered to see if it was to be peace or war'. Mrs Hossack presided at this meeting, and Constance Andrews spoke about the proposal for a census boycott. Plans were already far enough advanced for branch member Mrs Stansfield to be asking women to let her know if they would refuse to fill in their schedules (i.e. census resistance), or would go elsewhere on that night to evade the requirement to do so. From that time, Constance Andrews and the other active members of the branch were involved in a whirlwind of arrangements, fixing meetings and speakers, and deciding on the final format for their protest on census night.

Meanwhile the general arrangements for the census were being put in place. In Ipswich, the Superintendent Registrar of Births, Marriage and Deaths, Mr F.C. Ward, was to be in charge – his third census as supervisor – and similar government officials were appointed throughout Suffolk. The population of Ipswich was expected to be about 75,000, compared to 66,630 in 1901. The timetables were set, so that the enumerators would take out all the forms in the last days of March, and were expected to collect them in on 3 and 4 April.

Given the controversy being reflected in the national newspapers, the local papers were naturally interested in what local suffragettes might do and covered a meeting held by the WFL at the Old Museum Rooms on 16 March 1911. This meeting, which was said to have a large attendance, was presided over once more by Ipswich suffragette Mrs Hossack. In her opening remarks, she spoke of how women wanted the vote in order to be able to right wrongs, and stated the national WFL position that they would refuse to work with any political party until the vote was won. Mrs Nevinson, a national WFL speaker, acknowledged that it was a shocking thing to boycott something as important as the census, but the government had brought it upon itself; although it was a rebellious and even revolutionary act, it was still passive resistance. She added: 'the Census of 1911 will stand for all time as the protest of women against the Government.'[5]

In the discussion following the speeches, various suggestions were made as to how women might make their protest – by staying with a householder prepared to refuse to complete the schedule,and sharing the payment of any fine with her, or by going to all-night parties. Alternatively, Constance Andrews invited women to come to the WFL offices in Ipswich which would be open all night.

Two further meetings of the Ipswich WFL took place as census day approached. Presumably the women analysed what the action was about, what the risks were and saw to the finer details of the arrangements. They would have imagined different scenarios, and reassured women that they were not doing anything illegal. At some point the Old Museum Rooms were hired for the night, and Constance Andrews contacted women who might like to join in to say that if they were unable to stay up all night, they could go to the WFL offices next door in Arcade Street and sleep.[6]

As census night approached, Laurence Housman, who had been so involved in the development of the ideas and design of the action, included public meetings at both Bury St Edmunds (on 29 March 1911) and at Ipswich Co-op Hall (on 30 March) in his nationwide tour. Local branch member, Isobel Tippett of Wetherden, chaired both these meetings, and Mrs How Martin from the national WFL also attended. It was reported in the *Evening Star* that at the Ipswich meeting, where Constance Andrews was also present, Laurence Housman spoke 'for about an hour with great force and eloquence with no notes, arousing the enthusiasm and amusement of the audience'.[7] He is reported to have said, 'There are two forms of Government in this country – representative government for men, and non-representative government for women.' He felt that boycotting the census was an honourable action to highlight the fact that women were governed without consent. Even now, he added, the action would be called off if the government gave time to the Conciliation Bill.

A part of the speech was directed at the census enumerators – how might the suffragettes evade the enumerators, and how were the enumerators going to make sure that any suffragette seeking to evade the census was going to be counted? Laurence Housman said of his meeting in Ipswich:

The local registrar sent all the collectors to hear what I had to say so that they might know how to circumvent us. You should have seen their faces when I expounded the Act to them. I should say they'd never read the Act in their lives ... You never saw such astonishment and perplexity on their faces when they found they had no right to touch the evaders ... or to force them to give information.[8]

He stressed the law relating to the enumerators' limited powers.

The lack of clarity about census regulations and the possible government response to the suffrage action is reflected in the *Daily Sketch*'s coverage of the issue. On 15 March 1911 the paper wrote that there were reports that the census authorities might change the rules so that each woman would become the temporary occupier of the house where she was staying (thus making evasion by staying in a friend's house an offence); also that if women hired halls for all-night events, the halls might be treated as temporary dwelling-places (again making it an offence if women refused to complete the schedule). Such changes to the law may or may not have been seriously considered, but such reports would have made it even more important that local meetings explained the position in detail, and reassured potential evaders.

## Risks in joining the census boycott

By the time it came to Sunday, 2 April 1911, the stakes must have seemed quite high. Women had many issues to weigh up in deciding whether to join the action, and there may have been some who decided that it was not for them.

A census boycott was, after all, an unprecedented action, and no one knew exactly what would happen if they did not complete the schedule. It was clearly an offence to resist, the penalty for which could be prosecution and a £5 fine. However, there would have been worries that evading might also prove to be an offence, despite the assurances of suffragette advisers, especially as enumerators appeared unsure of their powers.

The decision to perform an act of civil disobedience is unlikely to be taken lightly by people who are generally law-abiding. This was perhaps even more difficult for families living in small villages where the enumerator might know them, and where they feared everyone might get to hear about an act of evasion. In places where there were just one or two suffragettes in a locality, support might also be hard to find. Indeed, Laurence Housman commented:

'I was struck by the extraordinary courage of women in small places in hostile populations ... it is one of the bravest things those small groups of women did because they did not know what the reaction would be.'[9] Women in employment might be particularly worried about their action becoming known, for fear of dismissal.

A woman would also find it difficult to stay away from home all night if her husband was not supportive. There might be children or other relatives to be cared for, or the husband might be absolutely opposed to women's suffrage. In fact, a woman might end up being compliant with the census when she had no wish to be, if her husband (or parent) insisted on including her in the schedule.

The idea of a woman being 'out all night' would have carried a greater significance in 1911 than now. Late-night partying was unknown at this time in the small towns of England, except perhaps in the privacy of one's own home. It would be very strange indeed to go out late in the evening expecting to stay up all night. There was no transport at that time of night, and very little by way of street light.

Finally, the ethical issues raised in previous days must have had their effect. Many women may not have been absolutely convinced of the rightness of the census boycott, finding it hard to get a clear view through the complexity of the issues. It was certainly easier not to get too involved, and, therefore, the courage of those who did was even more remarkable.

## Census night – what happened elsewhere?

The national branches of the Women's Freedom League (WFL) and Women's Political and Social Union (WSPU) naturally wanted to attract maximum publicity for their action, and various public events took place in London. The national newspapers thought this excellent copy, and reported widely on these events, including several pages of photos.

The main WFL event was to walk and talk at midnight in Trafalgar Square. No rally was planned; it was simply a gathering of census resisters and evaders who took the opportunity to talk about the reasons for their action to each other and any of the public who were out and about. They accompanied this by a large poster campaign throughout London with activists putting up papers saying, 'No Vote, No Census' throughout the small hours.

The WSPU had a full schedule of events, starting at 8 p.m. at the Aldwych Skating Rink with a concert of music by the suffragette composer,

Dr Ethel Smyth. The programme included the 'March of the Women', the song that Ethel Smyth had composed and which had been taken on as the WSPU anthem in January of that year. All the main suffragette leaders were there, including Emmeline and Christabel Pankhurst, and Mr and Mrs Pethwick-Lawrence. Then the Actresses' Franchise League had a line-up of famous actresses performing plays, and there was more music and singing. Roller-skating and games went on until morning. The *Daily Sketch* reported the next day that over 1,000 women were there although differing amounts, both more and less, were given by other papers. There was a great deal of coming and going, including to a restaurant near Drury Lane which stayed open all night, and where people could get a meal served by WSPU members. There were similar all-night parties and events in other large cities throughout the country.

Travelling all night seemed a good option to some, and several suffragettes hired horse-drawn caravans which they used to travel around London, publicising their intent to evade the census. One group arrived at Trafalgar Square around midnight, before making their way as far as Putney Heath. They were awakened in the morning by various police officers who did not know what to do. Before they could decide, the horses were harnessed and the caravans moved off, returning to London via Downing Street (where they delivered the paper *Votes for Women* to the prime minister).[10] A picture of ten women in two caravans on Wimbledon Common holding placards saying 'No Vote No Census' led the front page of the *Daily Sketch* on 4 April.

What became clear in the press reports was that the police and enumerators were out counting women. Some instances were reported of women and supportive men being counted several times as they publicly moved about London. Others declared themselves 'red herrings' and professed that, whilst the police focused on them, thousands of other women were taking action in unseen places.

One of the most prevalent forms of evasion was to go and sleep at another woman's house, and the press was full of incidents and pictures of houses packed tight with women trying their best to get some sleep. This was a common form of protest across the whole country. *The Vote* reported: 'the hostess took us to room after room where directly the light was switched on heads rose from all over the floor presenting the oddest sight imaginable.'[11]

Those resisting (refusing to complete their census schedules) were exposed to possible prosecution. By definition many remain unknown, but others were proud to say what they had put on their schedules. Some of these statements were reported in *Votes for Women*: 'As I am a woman, and women do not count in the State, I refuse to be counted'; 'Dumb Politically, Blind to the Census, Deaf to the Enumerator'; or 'If I am intelligent enough to fill in this form, I can surely put an X on a ballot paper'.[12]

## Census night in Ipswich

The main publicised action for the Ipswich area was an all-night 'party' planned by Constance Andrews and the other women of the Ipswich WFL. It was held at the Old Museum Rooms and, according to the press, about thirty women attended.

It is not clear what exactly the Old Museum Rooms at No. 13 Museum Street, Ipswich, were used for in 1911. Originally, the building was purpose-built as Ipswich's first museum, but the exhibits soon outgrew the space, and, in 1857, the museum moved to its current site in High Street. For many years, early in the twentieth century, the building belonged to H.E. Archer, auctioneer,[13] and he rented out rooms to organisations for their meetings to be held. It was perhaps a surprise to Mr Archer when the WFL asked to hire the rooms for the whole night.

Afterwards, in the mid-twentieth century, the Old Museum Rooms became a dance hall and then lay derelict for many years until its refurbishment as a restaurant in the early part of the twenty-first century. There is much about the original design still to be seen – a large room downstairs, and a similarly large room upstairs with a mezzanine floor on three sides. We do not know whether these spaces were divided into smaller rooms, or if the women held their all-night event upstairs or downstairs. There does appear to have been activity downstairs, as an Ipswich *Evening Star* reporter had this to say when he passed by at midnight: 'They had a grand fire in the huge grate of the lower hall, and round it were gathered a small knot of women ...'[14]

From the press reports, it seems that it was about 6 p.m. on Sunday, 2 April 1911 that women started to arrive at the Old Museum Rooms. Women from Felixstowe and Hadleigh arrived first – perhaps because public transport was unavailable later. As the evening went on, the Ipswich women joined them. There was a varied group – women who would have to work the next day, some better-off women, mothers leaving their children at home for the night, women perhaps whose husbands were less supportive and women whose menfolk had come with them to keep guard at the door.

Despite the bright lights and the warm, blazing fire that would certainly be needed on a night in early April, and despite the community of women, there must have been some trepidation. No one actually knew what would happen. The information had been clear that it was not against the law to evade the census by being away from home, but the enumerators had seemed quite determined at Laurence Housman's meeting. The women may not have been entirely sure of the consequences of not complying with the law. This was not London, after all, with its large supportive group of women who had wealth and influence, many of whom had already been to prison. This was Ipswich, and no one in the group had been sent to prison for any action connected with suffrage; this was in fact their first action of this kind. With the exception of Hortense Lane's tax resistance, their demand for the vote had been made known through meetings, propaganda, fairs, and demonstrations. This was protest of a different order.

The lateness of the hour would not have helped. They were not used to staying up so late and many were a long way from home. The streets were dark, and despite the lights and the fire in the Old Museum Rooms, there would be shadows everywhere. At all their public meetings there were hecklers and abusers – might they turn up and make the night even more difficult? Doubtless it was a nervous group of women gathered there.

The enumerators and the police were certainly out and watching what happened. At some point an enumerator took the opportunity to count the women, because his book records that sixteen women and five men were at the Old Museum Rooms that night, with the word 'suffragettes' in brackets after the entry so there could be no doubt as to who was being counted.[15] The *Suffolk Chronicle* reported that the police counted twenty-three women out in the morning.[16] We cannot know exactly how many women, and men, came and went from the Old Museum rooms that night but these records do reveal that it was a considerable number, and that the enumerator and the police were watching.

Indeed, the report below suggests that the enumerators had entered into some sort of battle with the suffragettes:

> One enumerator was jubilant because he had captured a noted suffragette. It happened in this wise. The lady went to the now famous Museum St revels, but apparently thought better of the matter, returned home about midnight and her husband duly entered her on the schedule. It appears that the police were watching the Museum rooms and Suffragette offices the whole of Sunday night and took note of who left on Monday morning.[17]

Note the use of the words 'jubilant' and 'captured'.

Many of these women knew each other well. They had worked together to organise the action, arranging meetings and chairing and speaking at them. Some had arranged many other suffrage events together over the last couple of years, and some were also members of the Independent Labour Party and perhaps other organisations. We can assume that they supported each other, and lent each other hope and energy whenever one flagged.

According to Constance Andrews' report in *The Vote*, 'our party in the Old Museum Rooms was a great success. Games, recitations and songs made the night appear to vanish and when dawn streamed in upon us it saw bright faces and heard happy laughter.'[18] More details are given in her *Evening Star* report:

As no Census paper had been left at the Old Museum Rooms we were jubilant, for this meant that there was no legal difficulty ... All our party having arrived, we had supper ... then coffee at 4.30am and a hearty breakfast at 7am. After supper we assumed various disguises in case of intruders appearing. Some of the younger members of the party looked very ancient, and some others more youthful than usual. Hiding places were arranged in case of any official appearing. Speeches and songs were now the rule and all began to enter with zest into the spirit of the thing. The keynote of the speeches was a note of congratulation that all over the country we were keeping this anti-Census vigil. If we could have such a large gathering in Ipswich, how much greater would the numbers be in larger centres of population! Various examples of what was being done in Ipswich were mentioned – of how one unoccupied house was filled with Suffragettes for the night, and how exchanges were being effected. After the speeches came songs and recitations. By this time we had all reached a fairly high pitch of merriment and enthusiasm. We of course all joined heartily in our Suffragette Marseillaise, *The Awakening* ... There was an agreeable diversion in the shape of some weird ghost stories. After this our progressive whist drive began. Unlike other whist drives, there were no prizes, but the players all contributed to our cause. Those who did not take part in the drive read books, or played Patience which I think is rather an appropriate game for suffragettes. Next we kept the fun going by a series of charades in which everyone guessed the word Census. Having exhausted the possibilities of these diversions we started conundrums, and invited each other to spell words backwards. Some of the younger members of the party gave a capital exhibition of physical drill, which was much applauded. People began to leave to catch trains and go to work quite early, and after breakfast there was a gradual dispersal.[19]

Constance Andrews refers to the WFL song 'The Awakening', composed by Teresa del Riego earlier in the year, and it is also likely that the group sang the WSPU anthem 'The March of the Women', which had been written by Ethel Smyth at about the same time. A special song was put together for the night called the 'Census Song', which was to be sung to the tune of the 'British Grenadiers'. The middle verse went:

Whene'er we are commanded
To fill our papers in
We tear them up and burn them
For we don't care a pin
Then those who want the census
Must please to make a note
With a tow row row row row row
We first must have the vote![20]

A slight mystery surrounds the issue of whether there were other actions in and around Ipswich. In the *Evening Star* on the same day as Constance Andrews' report, there was a piece from two Ipswich WSPU suffragettes, Grace Roe and Lillie Roe (no relation):

There never was a whist drive, and there never was any intention of having a whist drive. It was a red herring across the track ... You see, we had secured the upstairs of the Old Museum rooms just as a blind, and had lots of chairs and tables taken in ... We had left the lights turned up in the various suffragette offices, to convey the idea that some of us were there, but bless you, we had all gone, and were scattered about all over the county.

Given the evidence of the enumerator's book – plus the fact that the WSPU weekly newspaper did not detail any other action in this area, and in fact specifically stated that Lillie Roe was at the Old Museum Rooms that night – this report may have been designed to create confusion for the authorities, or to make the action seem more varied and widespread than perhaps it was.

An unaccredited photograph in the *Suffolk Chronicle* entitled 'The Last Suffragette leaving the Old Museum Rooms' shows an almost deserted street with a single woman walking away.[21]

## Who was at the Old Museum Rooms?

The census schedules of 1911 only became available to the public in 2009. National suffrage historians Elizabeth Crawford and Jill Liddington set themselves the task of studying the schedules, and seeing what the suffragettes on their database of names in London and the rest of the country, actually did. Did they resist the census, evade it or comply with it?[22]

To their surprise, fewer suffragettes resisted or evaded the census than they expected. Even some of the most radical women who had been to prison, hunger struck and suffered forcible feeding, and then continued to campaign, complied in completing their schedules.

In their view, the reasons for this are not immediately apparent. As pointed out already, there were argued to be ethical issues concerning not completing the census; there were certainly risks of various kinds which would have an effect; and of course the wishes of women who were not householders in their own right might not be respected. However, such issues would surely not deter radical, militant suffragettes, some of whom had supportive and actively campaigning husbands. Liddington and Crawford propose two main reasons for this. Firstly, that where a family had suffered a number of child deaths, they may not have wished to evade or resist completing the census schedule. Their strongest feeling might have been that the government must have this information so that child mortality could be combated. The second main reason is based in the fact that their research showed very few employed women resisted or evaded; this suggests either that they feared losing their employment if they were discovered in an act of passive disobedience, or that, if they were low-paid workers, they might fear a fine they could not afford.

A further consideration, in my view, is that women might indeed have both attended census evasion events, and complied in completing the census schedule. A possible local example of this is the schedule of Lillie Roe, which shows her to have been at home in Fonnereau Road, Ipswich with her mother and a servant on census night. Yet it was she who wrote a report in the press, jointly with Grace Roe, saying she had been part of the census boycott, and was reported in *Votes for Women* to have been at the Old Museum Rooms. It seems feasible that women might have been very keen for the action to succeed, and be seen to succeed. They knew that visible numbers were important for publicity and so may well have attended the events but also wanted to complete, or be entered into, their schedules for various reasons. We do, moreover, have the evidence that indicates that at least one woman did go to the Old Museum Rooms before returning home within the counting period, and was entered on the schedule as a result. This could have occurred to more than one woman, including perhaps this one, reported in the *Suffolk Chronicle*:

> A woman was a lodger and as Census Day approached, she boldly intimated to her landlady that she didn't intend to supply information. The enumerator gave her a form of her own. When he called yesterday the landlady had filled up her paper, but the lodger's was blank. He was lucky enough to have called when she was at home ... Gently but firmly he informed her that she must fill up the form, and without a word of protest she filled it up, and signed it, as he put it, 'like a lamb'.[23]

It was not so easy to resist or evade when confronted by the enumerator.

Let us consider which of the women of Ipswich and the local area were at the Old Museum Rooms that night, and what their census schedules indicate, in as far as we can. Local and national suffrage newspapers mention some of the women by name, and we can make some reasonable assumptions about other women being there because they have been mentioned as taking part in the planning of the event and public meetings on the issue. It has not, however, been possible to find the census schedule for some, where their address is not known.[*]

*Women most likely at the Old Museum Rooms that night, and whose details do not appear on their census schedule*

**CONSTANCE ANDREWS** was secretary of the Ipswich Women's Freedom League, and the main organiser of the census evasion event at the Old Museum Rooms. She lived with her brother-in-law, George Pratt, and sister Lilla and their two sons in Norwich Road, Ipswich. Her name does not appear on the census schedule for this household, however. In fact, only George Pratt and the two sons George and Oliver appear. At the side of the form, the enumerator has written: 'There were two female suffragists in this family who went to some place unknown for the night. The female servant went with them.' We can assume that Lilla Pratt, who was often reported to be at suffrage meetings with her sister Constance, and a servant were also at the Old Museum Rooms.

---

[*] Further biographical details of the women, where known, are given in the Appendix.

**CATHERINE BASTIAN** and her husband, Henry, were strong suffrage supporters, and founded the Hadleigh branch of the WFL. In her report in *The Vote*, 15 April 1911, Constance says, 'It would be invidious to mention names, but an exception may be made in the case of our friend Mr Bastian, who nobly supported us.' I think we can safely assume that Catherine was also there.

Catherine and Henry Bastian do not appear to have completed their census schedule. The schedule lists only Henry Bastian, with very few details, and this is clearly not of his own volition, as where the schedule is normally signed by the householder, it has been signed by Charles Verlander, Registrar, Hadleigh. Above the signature it says: 'In accordance with instructions received from the census office (Mr Bastian having declined to give any information).'

**MARGARET FISON** was a WSPU member, reported in *Votes for Women* to have been at the Old Museum Rooms on census night.[24] She is not recorded on her household's census schedule, which shows the head of the household as Harry, aged 43, at home that night with two sisters, Alice and Edith, and two servants.

**MRS HOSSACK** had been involved in the suffrage campaign in Ipswich for many years. She presided at various WFL meetings discussing the action in the preceding weeks, so it is probably safe to assume that she was present. Her name does not appear on her household's census schedule, which lists only her husband James, their three children, Beatrice, Ian and Phillip, and two servants.

**EVELYN SPENCER KING** was the organiser of the WSPU shop in Dial Lane, Ipswich. She was reported to have been at the Old Museum Rooms on census night by *Votes for Women*. The census schedule of her household shows her father, Mr Spencer King, a widower, aged 74, at home with two servants that night. There is no mention of Evelyn on the schedule.

**ISOBEL TIPPETT** was a WFL member from Wetherden who chaired the Laurence Housman meetings at both Bury St Edmunds and at Ipswich. The rather confusing census schedule for her household does not appear to have an entry either for herself or her husband, but shows her two young sons at home with their grandmother. It is highly likely that she was at the Old Museum Rooms, and perhaps he was one of the men who guarded the door with Mr Bastian.

*Women reported to be at the Old Museum Rooms that night*

**MISS ELVEY** was also a WSPU member, reported in *Votes for Women* to have been at the census action. No details of her full name or address have been found, so it has not been possible to look at her census schedule.

**LILLIE ROE** was an active member of the WSPU in Ipswich. She was reported to be at the census action at the Old Museum rooms in *Votes for Women*, though, as we have seen, she also gave an interview with Grace Roe to the *Evening Star* the next day saying the event had not really taken place, and instead they had been 'scattered about all over the county'. However, Lillie Roe appears on her household schedule, which was completed by her 76-year-old mother, raising one of the mysteries of Ipswich's census night.

*Other active local suffragettes*

**PHYLLIS PEARCE** is not mentioned in press reports at the time of the census action, but was active in the local WSPU. Her household's census schedule does not mention her name – it records Arthur (head) and Alice (his wife) and a son (aged 24).

**HEPHZIBAH STANSFIELD** was a WFL member who had, at meetings leading up to the action, encouraged women to let her know what they intended to do on census night. We also know that her husband had supported women's suffrage for many years. However, their census schedule is complete – perhaps because he was an art teacher at a local school, and feared losing his job.

**ADA MATTHEW** was the secretary of the Hadleigh branch of the WFL, and lived next door to Catherine and Henry Bastian. She was said to be very hard-working in the suffrage cause locally. Her census schedule shows her to be compliant. She appears on the form completed by her mother, who was 71 years old at this time. It is interesting that of all the local census forms that have come to light in relation to suffragettes, this is the only one where there were child deaths in the family. Mrs Matthew, a widow, had lost two of her five children. Might this, as Crawford and Liddington propose, be the factor that made Ada Matthew compliant, and if so, did it prevent her going to the census action that night?

**LAURA CAY** was a member of the WSPU, and helped organise meetings during this time. Her census schedule shows her to be compliant. Her mother, aged 80, completed the form.

**HORTENSE LANE** was a WFL member who had already been prosecuted for refusing to pay taxes until the vote was won. A month after the census action, she appeared in court alongside Constance for further tax refusal. Her husband was said to be a suffrage supporter. However, their census schedule shows her to be compliant. Her friend, Dr Elizabeth Knight, in London on census night, was a resister.

**GRACE ROE** was the leader of the WSPU in Ipswich. She was a lodger at the time, living in the home of Thomas Everard, printer, in Silent Street. Although a boarder is mentioned on that household's census schedule, the name of Grace Roe is not there. The action at the Old Museum Rooms included many WSPU members, but, given her newspaper report quoted previously, we cannot say for sure that she was there.

In her report, Constance Andrews says that the women of Felixstowe arrived first. We do not know who these women might be. In January 1911, *The Vote* said Miss Milano was hoping to form a WFL branch – perhaps she was there.*

## The success of the census action

Did the Ipswich women contribute to a successful action? There are various aspects to consider. These include: whether the action deprived the government of the information it was seeking in its census; whether it placed additional pressure on parliament to enfranchise women; and whether it provided worthwhile publicity for the 'Votes for Women' campaign, and drew more women to it.

The census action certainly worried the government enough for it to consider carefully the action that the women were taking. They must have been relieved indeed when the National Union of Women's Suffrage Societies declared its opposition to the boycott, because then it knew that thousands of

---

* An interesting footnote is that Dr Elizabeth Garrett Anderson, now in her 70s and living back in Aldeburgh, who had started that first Ladies' Petition back in 1866 demanding the vote, does not, according to Liddington and Crawford, appear to have completed her census schedule.

non-militant suffragists in every town in the country would not be joining in. Nevertheless, it took its own bureaucratic measures to minimise large-scale census inaccuracy, and ensure the count would not be nullified by the protest. John Burns, the minister responsible for the census, wrote in a memo to the Home Secretary, Winston Churchill on 28 March 1911:

> The Registrar-general who is responsible for the census does not propose to force matters unduly and will be satisfied if he can obtain an estimate of the number of persons who congregate in the buildings referred to (i.e. places suffragettes designated for mass evasion).[25]

This would explain the presence of the police and enumerators out and about in Ipswich, as in London and doubtless many other towns, doing their best to count boycotting women, even if this was of doubtful accuracy and did not provide any detailed information.

In the ensuing days, the government and the suffrage organisations disputed whether the boycott had been successful in this interesting polemical game. Of course, the WSPU and the WFL claimed that it was an enormous success, and its newspapers were full of accounts of the actions in London and across the country. They were bolstered by the widespread coverage in the national press. There was also a 'hidden' aspect to the campaign – resisters may simply have refused to complete their forms without taking part in any more public event; also many women spent the night in each other's houses, and were again not visible. Moreover, the suffrage organisations had previously stated that if there were very few resisters, the government would make an example of them by prosecuting them, but if there were many, they would not. Accordingly the lack of any prosecutions actually lent support to their claims.

On 5 April 1911, only two days after the enumerators had gathered in the census schedules, a question was asked in parliament by MP Ian Malcolm as to 'whether the suffragette agitation against the census is likely to affect prejudicially the accuracy of our statistics'. John Burns replied that the number of individuals who had evaded the census was 'altogether negligible', and as regards any possible prosecution, 'in the hour of success mercy and magnanimity must be shown'.[26] It was a patronising response that must have angered the women very much. The suffrage press fought back by reminding people that they had said that if the action was hugely successful, the authorities would not add further publicity to the cause by prosecuting resisters. Moreover, the courts were already tied up with women who had been arrested in other actions, filling women's prisons where they refused to eat. The government would prefer to claim that it had just been a very few women to avoid further prosecutions. And this is precisely what happened. Both sides were manipulating what little was known in the interest of their own cause.

We now know from the work of Liddington and Crawford that the issue of census schedule completion was perhaps more complex than was acknowledged at the time. There were unexpected reasons why some suffragettes, who one would fully expect to join the boycott, in fact complied and filled out the census. Even in the small number of schedules found in relation to the Ipswich women, such questions are raised. Perhaps in fact the suffrage organisations were fully aware that the action had not been successful in terms of depriving the government of the information it required, but were happy enough at the publicity that it generated. It was obvious by this time that no single action was going to lead to suffrage, so perhaps this one would be regarded, like many others, as part of a gathering momentum which would ultimately lead to that goal. The suffrage organisations did not dwell on the argument, but began to turn their minds to their next event.

Judged on the publicity engendered, however, the census boycott was very successful. When it was suggested, the suffragettes could have had no idea that it would provoke so much debate, or even antagonism, not only from the conservative elements in the country, but also from the liberal intelligentsia who were normally supportive of their claim. It allowed them, in the columns and letter pages of national newspapers and in public meetings throughout the country, to develop their ideas about citizenship, about what representative government was and about exclusion from democracy. These debates would have been held at the dinner tables of families everywhere. Families interested in suffrage had to decide what to do.

People who up to now had shown little interest in the suffrage cause, might well have reflected on that sentence, 'If women don't count, don't count women'. and begun for the first time to wonder about their lack of a political voice. Some would have looked again at the Conciliation Bill, which the government had steadfastly refused to find time for in the parliamentary programme, and seen that it demanded little more than that women who already had the municipal vote should have a parliamentary vote, and wondered whether they did not have a good cause.

Moreover, unlike many suffrage campaigns, this was not confined to London or the main cities. Like in Ipswich, people in towns and villages across the country were caught up in this brave act, and the fact that the women involved were local would have caused more talk (or gossip perhaps) than many other actions thus far.

Constance Andrews could have derived some quiet satisfaction from her leadership of an action that involved so many local women, and so much publicity. For women with very little power, there must have been a certain exhilaration in outwitting the authorities. But basically she, like the leaders of all the suffrage organisations, did not dwell on the outcomes. She did not have time, because within three weeks she was standing in Woodbridge magistrates' court.

# 5

# THE BUSY YEAR CONTINUES

## No Vote, No Tax

At the beginning of January 1911, Constance Andrews, along with her friends Hortense Lane and Dr Elizabeth Knight, refused to buy a dog licence. They were inspired by the 'No Vote, No Tax' campaign. In April, the law caught up with them.

The Women's Tax Resistance League (WRTL) had been created to advise on these actions. Its inaugural meeting had taken place in October 1909 in the London drawing room of Louisa, daughter of Suffolk's Dr Elizabeth Garrett Anderson. The latter was also there, still fighting for equality for women despite being in her 70s. Although it was a separate organisation, the WRTL saw itself as working within the remit of the Women's Freedom League (WFL), encouraging tax evasion and offering detailed tax advice. The words 'tax evasion' did not carry the controversial meaning that they do now. On the contrary, the driving motivation for the league was to challenge (in a similar way to the census action) the unconstitutional nature of a system which made women pay taxes when they had no say in how they were spent. At first, the league intended to help working women evade income tax and inhabited house duty. But more popular and straightforward was the refusal to pay the annual tax on dogs, carriages, male servants, armorial bearings and so on. These protests were begun and over within a few months, whereas withholding income and property taxes took place over a long period of time, and publicity was hard to sustain.

The actions of local suffragette tax resisters were very similar to those of hundreds of others across the country. Chapter 3 described Hortense Lane's refusal to pay her Inhabited House Duty in 1909, and how local suffragettes made the court case and subsequent auction of seized goods an opportunity for meetings promoting their cause. In 1911, Constance Andrews joined in, and her refusal to pay her fine alongside her friends enhanced the drama.

'No Taxation Without Representation' campaigns have a long history. Back in 1637 John Hampden refused to pay 'ship money', a tax controversially imposed by King Charles I at a time when parliament had not sat for ten years. Ultimately, this was a precipitating factor in the crisis leading to the English Civil War. The Women's Tax Resistance League had as its logo a ship on the sea, remembering this heritage. Ironically, Hampden's native town of Aylesbury erected a statue in his honour in 1913 – at the same time as women were being imprisoned for tax refusal.

On 20 April, Constance Andrews appeared at Woodbridge magistrates' court charged with not having a dog licence. Hortense Lane and Dr Elizabeth Knight were also charged with this offence, and with not purchasing licences for their carriages as well. Did Constance Andrews really have a dog which she kept at Hortense Lane's farm in Witnesham? If she had kept a dog at her home in Norwich Road, she would have appeared at an Ipswich Court. It is possible that Hortense Lane signed over to Constance one of her dogs for this specific purpose. The police reported that when they visited the farm, there were seven dogs – four had licences and three did not.[1] Of these three, it was said that a dog belonged to each of Constance, Hortense and Elizabeth Knight. Asked by the magistrate why she had kept the dog unlawfully, Constance replied, 'I don't call it unlawful. I am not a person in the eyes of the law. Therefore I refuse to pay a licence.' When asked if she now intended to pay for the licence, she said she did not: 'Taxation and representation ought to go hand in hand.' She was given the opportunity to say more, and replied:

> I do not wish to defend myself, but wish to ask you if you from the Bench would send up to the Prime Minister a request that The Government should pass the Conciliation Bill for women's suffrage. If benches of magistrates would do that, it would have a great effect and you would not have any more trouble with the suffragists.

Constance was fined £1 with 8s 8d costs, and told that if she did not pay, goods would be seized to that amount or she would go to prison for seven days. Hortense Lane and Elizabeth Knight were also fined.

All three women refused to pay their fines, and held a public meeting outside the court which was well received by a 'small crowd'.

Early in May, Hortense Lane and Elizabeth Knight had their farm wagon (called a 'waggon' at this time) seized by bailiffs in lieu of their fines and it was sold by auction in Woodbridge. Local suffragettes turned it into a publicity event, as before. The *East Anglian Daily Times* report states that the wagon:

> Bore the names of Knight and Lane ... Whilst the usual auctioneering went on, the Women's Freedom League made the waggon their headquarters for the day, and used the time to sell papers to the crowd ... Constance Andrews, who was also fined, has deprived herself of all her goods and awaits arrest.[2]

Constance had gifted all her possessions to her sister Lilla to prevent the bailiffs from meeting the fine by seizing and selling her possessions. A few days later, on 20 May, the police went to her home in Norwich Road and, on being told she was in town, went looking for her. She was in the Mechanics Union, now the Ipswich Institute, with her friend Lillie Roe, and the police arrested her and took her straight to prison.

At that time, Ipswich's prison was in Grimwade Street. Constance was held for a week in the 2nd Division alongside women sentenced for criminal offences. The prison records show that she was one of a small number of women in the gaol at that time.[3] There was a 15-year-old girl on her way to a reformatory after stealing a gold watch. There were two working women of a similar age to Constance – one serving fourteen days for stealing money, and one serving twenty-eight days for being drunk and disorderly. Perhaps she found the whole situation appalling – she was, after all, a law-abiding woman in her late 40s who had significant roles in public life. The *East Anglian Daily Times* reporter described her as 'a lady of culture and well versed in today's social questions, especially regarding women's industry. She represents women's labour on the Trades Council and was one of the Reception Committee for TUC Conference 18 months ago.'[4] On the other hand, we know that she was committed to these causes, as with her suffrage activities, because she wanted to improve life for everyone, particularly women. It is likely that she would have been interested in the stories of the other women in the prison, learning about their lives and telling them of the hope that suffrage would bring.

From her prison record we learn that Constance Andrews was five foot and half an inch tall, and had dark brown hair. She is not recorded as having any occupation. She was apparently able to wear her own clothes, read her own books and have vegetarian food brought in by her sister Lilla. We are told that she had breakfast at 5 a.m., and then had spells of reading, chapel, exercise and visits. On her release, it was said:

> ... she was not longing for martyrdom ... the work one did outside was incomparably harder than sitting in a prison cell. As far as Ipswich Prison went, it was very clean, well-ventilated, and everything was as good as a prison could be though very little air came in. The only thing she minded was being shut in at night, and when the door was locked one felt a little tiny bit lonely ... All she saw was kindly faces [here she compares her situation with the privations and torture which other suffragettes experience in prison].[5]

Perhaps what she said in public did not reflect her entire experience. Her friend, Bess Boyd-Brown, recalled these interesting details more than sixty years later:

> She said to me after her release, 'Betty, it was terrible' ... We all went to see her come out at 8am down Grimwade St, and as she came out, this girl said 'I'm going to throw stones at her.' And Constance just turned round and said 'Good morning, Emily', and she said 'Good morning, Miss Andrews'. Then we had a meeting at night. I said to her, 'What was the worst time?' and she said when she was locked in at night. She always suffered from imagination. She couldn't bear to be in enclosed spaces ... She laughed after, she said 'I did one good thing, I converted the Wardress ...' I said were they kind to her and she said, 'Yes, as much as they could be.' ... She was such a gentle person, you'd think she would be blown away almost, and yet she had all this strength.[6]

Hundreds of women across the country had been to prison as part of their campaign to get the vote over the previous seven or eight years, and a tradition had grown up that local suffragettes would meet them at the prison gates on their release. This was partly to acknowledge and celebrate their action, and to offer support – some women would be traumatised and some weak and ill through hunger striking and forcible feeding – and also, of course, to gain maximum publicity. Constance Andrews' release was no exception. A delegation came from London, headed by the WFL president, Charlotte Despard, and joined the local suffragettes outside the prison gates. Pictures show Charlotte Despard, Mrs Hossack and Constance in an open-topped cab, with many people standing around – suffragettes, well-wishers, onlookers, and the police. After greeting her, the cab, surrounded by people walking, some holding the WFL banner 'Dare To Be Free', made its way through St Helen's Street, Carr Street, and Tavern Street before turning into Museum Street where a celebratory breakfast was held at the WFL office at No. 16 Arcade Street.

The local press report mentions that London suffragettes, Miss Sidley and Mrs Sainty, also came. Locally, Constance's close suffragette friends were there – Catherine Bastian, Mrs Hossack, Isobel Tippett, Lilla Pratt, Lillie Roe and others. Grace Roe of the Women's Social and Political Union (WSPU) called in to congratulate her, and apparently there were comparisons of different prison conditions amongst the women with Charlotte Despard declaring that the food in Holloway 'was horrid'.

The first to speak formally at the breakfast was Mrs Hossack. She praised the women who not only gave their time and acumen to the cause, but also gave up their liberty. Constance Andrews was one of these:

... they had known her as a great worker, but now by her imprisonment she had made a stronger protest for equal rights than ever she had done previously. Women had shown that they dared to be free, and that to gain that freedom they were willing to give up liberty, and win it through the prison gates.

Mrs Despard also paid a tribute to Constance Andrews saying that:

She had known Constance personally, and of the fine work she had done before there was any Freedom League. She knew how deeply and passionately she felt the distressing things that went on in the world. Things would not be better until men and women stood together in the community.

Constance Andrews was reported throughout to be in 'excellent spirits'.[7]

## An Englishwoman's Home ...

On 10 May, in the period between Constance Andrews' trial and imprisonment, Grace Roe's WSPU hired the Lyceum, and with London colleagues from the Actresses' Franchise League, staged two plays – *The Apple* by Inez Bensusan and *An Englishwoman's Home* by Mr Arncliffe-Sennett, the husband of a prominent London suffragette. The Lyceum in Carr Street was at that time Ipswich's most popular theatre, and had a seating capacity of over 1,000.

Neither of the plays performed at the Lyceum in May 1911 would find space in a theatre programme now, except in a retrospective, but nevertheless they are not without interest. Inez Bensusan had previous experience as an actress in Australia and in 1908 she was one of the founding members of the Actresses' Franchise League. By 1911 she was in charge of the League's play department and her first play, *The Apple*, was about a family of three sisters and their brother.[8] The latter is the apple of his father's eye, and the sisters' needs are regarded as inferior to his. They struggle for their livelihoods and independence whilst the resources of the family are lavished on him. The story centres on the sister Helen, who resigns from her secretarial job when her superior makes sexual advances towards her. She wants to use her share of the family's estate to emigrate – only to discover that it has been given to her brother, who is squandering it. Helen has to return to her superior; whether as his secretary or his 'mistress' is left ambiguous, and the one-act play ends on an extremely pessimistic note. Even a hundred years later we can feel the sense of entitlement of the father and son, and the bitter anger of Helen and her sisters that this play was designed to portray.

By contrast, *An Englishwoman's Home* is a mixture of slapstick drama and more serious reflection.[9] It focuses on the sphere of working-class women, and delineates a situation that may still be familiar to some women today – having to work and also do everything in the house, even when the husband is unemployed. In the play, John has been out of work for a year, but refuses to do any 'women's work'. Maria does charring, takes in washing, and looks after the male lodger, the baby and the house. She is invited to a suffragette meeting and leaves the baby with her husband – resulting in some highly amusing moments as he proves ignorant of how to do the most basic parenting tasks. In this play, political activity is seen as empowering for women, with getting the vote providing the answer to many problems.

Local Ipswich suffragettes made a great day out of the performance of these two plays.[10] Grace Roe, Margaret Fison, Evelyn King and Lillie Roe, amongst others, had decorated the whole of the Lyceum in the WSPU colours of green, purple and white. Banners were slung from the balconies. Mrs Pethwick-Lawrence, a prominent suffragette in the national movement, and a great friend and co-worker of Emmeline Pankhurst, chaired the event, and several well-known suffragettes came from London to take on the acting roles. The sense of occasion was completed by children dancing and music from an orchestra.

In the publicity for the event, it was said that there would be a 'ladies' orchestra' to be conducted by Lewis Taylor, the Lyceum's musical director. However, reports of the day itself reveal that it was a mixed orchestra that performed. At this time, women were not allowed to play in orchestras – it was thought they did not have the strength or the stamina. Moreover, women did not play woodwind or percussion as apparently they looked ugly when doing so. Suffragette musicians had started to challenge this, but perhaps in Ipswich it was not possible on this occasion to find a complete set of female players. Nevertheless, even if men were needed to fill some gaps, it would have been an exciting event for female instrumental players in the town.

An interesting sentence in the press report reminds us of the context: 'There was nothing militant about the proceedings – not even in the speech of Mrs Pethwick-Lawrence who was in a jubilant mood over prospects of a woman's suffrage bill.'

There had just been an extremely successful vote in the House of Commons regarding suffrage. Since the government had not included a bill in their programme for this session of parliament, the option of a private member's bill had been taken. George Kemp MP agreed to put his name to what was in effect the Conciliation Bill and, only a few days before Mrs Pethwick-Lawrence came to Ipswich, it had been passed with 255 MPs voting for a limited amount of women's suffrage, on the same terms as men, and only 88 against. The feeling amongst suffragettes was that it was only a matter of months before they would be given the vote. It is hard for us to understand how hopeful they were, knowing as we do that years of increasing militant activity still lay ahead, with harsh responses from the government. But the women lived in hope and occasionally, as in the early summer of 1911, had good reason to believe that by the time the year was out, they would have the vote.

The events at the Lyceum must have been successful because, on 29 June 1911, the WFL put on two plays by Isabel Tippett at one of Ipswich's other theatres, the Hippodrome in Saint Nicholas' Street, which had been 'put at their disposal' by the manager.

We already know Isabel Tippett as a committed suffragette who had been closely associated with Constance Andrews and the WFL for a couple of years.[11] Although it has not been possible to find any of her plays, she must have been regarded as a writer of some note, for the local reporter says that 'the plays performed in Ipswich that day were premiers so far as England is concerned, but they have already been performed on the Riviera, and been favourably commented on by English and Continental critics'.[12]

*In Search of Adventure* was about a young rich girl who, according to the report, wishes to marry for love rather than for her position in society. *To Fit the Case* was a slighter, funnier piece, again about the impossibility of imagining any other future for a young girl than marriage. These plays appear to have been acted by members of the local WFL with support from the Actresses' Franchise League. Children danced in the interval and Constance Andrews' brother-in-law, George Pratt, conducted a 'ladies' orchestra'.

In between these artistic events, the Women's Coronation Procession of 16 June 1911 took place. Edward VII had enjoyed just a short reign, and now George V was to be crowned. Anxious to be visibly identified with the patriotism displayed at such times, and as usual using an event to get across their own message, this procession was a joyous occasion, fuelled by the suffragettes' feeling that success and the end of their campaign were imminent. About 40,000 women walked through London during this fabulously colourful event, with many different sections representing women workers, the different suffrage organisations and local branches with their own banners. The procession was headed up by a Pageant of Famous Women – Joan of Arc, for example, and Grace Darling. We are told that Grace Roe led out a contingent of Ipswich WSPU members under two banners designed by Ipswich member Ada Ridley. Isabel Tippett led the Ipswich and Hadleigh WFL groups with their banners.

Constance Andrews was in a special part of the procession dedicated to women who had been to prison for their beliefs. By this time, there were about 700 such women. Each carried a silver pennant and walked in front of a banner showing a woman with a broken chain in her hands and the words 'From Prison to Citizenship'. Constance's friend, Bess Boyd-Brown, gives a delightful account of the day when she mentions it in an interview some seventy years later:

Then they had the big suffragette procession in London and she invited my friend and I to go. She had to go in the front because she was with the prisoners to carry the banner. Then she took us – we were only working girls – and she took us to a hotel I don't know where it was – to lunch. Well, we thought it was the height of everything – marvellous. The only thing that worried me about that, I was worried about the mounted police. Their horses rose up like that and I thought they were coming to crush us, you see. But it was a marvellous day ... When we went to the hotel, I mean I tell you we were – I don't mean we were among the poorest of the poor, but we were hard up. She said 'What shall we have for lunch?' Florence who sat next to me – the menu was all in French! But she was very good, she said 'Well I think the best thing we can do is to have an omelette.' I wondered what it would be like but it was beautiful ... It's funny, my mother was very strict ... yet she allowed me to go to London with her ... she just said 'Well, if you'll be with Miss Andrews, then that's alright ...'[13]

In and amongst all this activity, the Ipswich suffragettes continued to build their local campaign. Meetings were held, newspapers sold, money collected, funds raised. National suffragettes came to town, including Millicent Fawcett (president of the NUWSS). Lord Lytton (chair of the Conciliation Committee) also came to speak at a public meeting. The WFL added more branches to its collection, at Elmsett and Stowmarket. The WSPU opened a shop at No. 2 Dial Lane, run by Evelyn King. Like the many other shops across the country, this one would display in its window the poster advertising the content of the week's newspaper – *Votes for Women*. It also showed various books and pamphlets about the cause and was carefully decorated in their colours. In addition to these, the people of Ipswich would be able to buy brooches, scarves and sashes as well as some of the board and card games the WSPU had invented. On one day a week they served afternoon tea, and also ran a suffrage library. It would have been an interesting addition to Ipswich's main street.

Perhaps a measure of the local success was the formation of a local anti-suffrage group. In such groups, women maintained that they did not need the vote. These women argued that finance, the military and trade formed the business of parliament and that, since women did not participate in these fields, they could not comment on them. They recommended that women should content themselves with the conduct of the home and their local community.

In November 1911, the government crushed the women's hopes. Prime Minister Asquith announced that there would be a Manhood Suffrage Bill in the next parliament which would give the remaining non-enfranchised men the vote. However, there was no mention of any vote for women. When pressed, he said that it was not impossible that there might be amendments that would grant limited suffrage to women. Unusually, he agreed to accept a deputation of nine women's suffrage societies but, after listening to the women, he reiterated that he did not support women's suffrage. Although he said that the House of Commons might decide otherwise, he would have known how unlikely it was that such a bill could be passed without government support.

The women's response was immediate and definite. A large group of suffragettes left Caxton Hall on 21 November for the House of Commons. After the usual police resistance, a breakaway group of women started to throw stones and smash government office windows – also those of hostile newspapers and West End stores. There were 223 arrests. A new phase of the campaign had begun.

Contemporary records do not say whether any Ipswich women were a part of this action. However, this may be what the composer, Michael Tippett, son of Isabel Tippett, was referring to when he wrote in his autobiography:

In 1911, the Liberal Government of Asquith reached the point of passing a women's suffrage bill in the House of Commons. But it was thrown out by the House of Lords and, as a result, all the suffragette organisations held a monster demonstration in Trafalgar Square ... my mother, who was participating, was arrested and sent briefly to prison.[14]

That such action was deeply empowering to women is clear from this newspaper article of 1958, which celebrated the fortieth anniversary of women getting the vote:

When she was about 18 Mrs Phyllis Cornell of 44 Westerfield Road, [Ipswich] widow of the chemist, often used to go to London to join Mrs Pankhurst's campaigns. Once she walked in a procession led by Mrs Pankhurst to Downing St. The women were set on smashing the Prime Minister's windows. 'When we got to the bottom of Downing Street the police lined the entrance three deep ... We charged them and broke through. There was a pitched battle in the street but it never got as far as Number 10.' On another occasion Mrs Cornell was chosen to throw a stone through a window in Whitehall. She had to choose her own stone and window. 'By the time I'd got a stone – not easy in Whitehall, a messenger ran up and said the House of Commons had risen. So the stone-throwing was called off.' ... Mrs Cornell said of Mrs Pankhurst that ... she was small and frail but her spirit as strong as iron. Mrs Cornell thought the suffragette struggle was worth it. 'After that everything seemed small, and one was afraid of nothing. The suffragette movement was the making of me.'[15]

# 6

# AND STILL NO VOTE

## The unceasing energy of the local suffragettes

The Ipswich campaign suffered a serious loss at the end of January 1912: Constance Andrews was voted onto the National Executive Committee of the Women's Freedom League (WFL) in London. It was a tribute to her hard work over many years of campaigning in Ipswich, as well as to the personal commitment shown by her willingness to go to prison. Her organising skills were immediately put to good use as she arranged and chaired national WFL meetings and events. A couple of months later, she travelled to Wales to meet branch secretaries there and offer them support and advice.[1] The heartfelt plea she had expressed in 1907 to be at the centre of things was now realised.

Her Ipswich campaigning colleagues must have felt proud. At first she tried to remain involved with the local group, and at their Annual General Meeting in February 1912 she was re-elected honorary secretary. However, by the late autumn it appears that her sister, Lilla Pratt, had stepped into her shoes.

Whilst the WFL nationally, with the help of Constance Andrews, was getting on with business as usual, the Women's Social and Political Union (WSPU) continued its more militant response to the disappointments the government had dealt its members at the end of the previous year. For the first time Emmeline Pankhurst, and therefore the WSPU, endorsed attacks on property. In a speech in February 1912 she said, 'If the argument of the stone, that time-honoured argument, is sufficient, then we will never use any stronger argument. And this is the weapon and the argument we are going to use next time.'[2] She spoke about the suffering of women, and made the point that when women demonstrated, and made deputations to Downing Street or the House of Commons they got 'battered about and insulted', whereas stone throwing resulted in a simple arrest. At the same time, she continued to write to Prime Minister Asquith to try and find a way forward, but he refused to meet with her.

On 1 March 1912, all the leaders of the WSPU went with their supporters to the West End of London and threw stones, breaking many shop windows. There were further waves of window breaking two days later, and the courts were forced to sit beyond their normal hours to deal with the number of cases. Emmeline Pankhurst, as always leading in action as well as word, was imprisoned alongside other leaders. After a few days, Mr and Mrs Pethwick-Lawrence were also arrested and charged alongside Emmeline Pankhurst with conspiracy to incite violence. This was the first time that all the main leaders had been in prison at the same time. Only Christabel Pankhurst managed to escape to France, and she conducted the campaign for the next couple of years from there.

The constitutionalists of Millicent Fawcett's National Union of Women's Suffrage Societies (NUWSS) were furious at the turn of events the WSPU had engineered which, they felt, could only antagonise those whose support they needed. They did not necessarily agree that Asquith's scuppering of the Conciliation Bill at the end of 1911 was terminal; they were continuing to try and achieve amendments to the Manhood Suffrage Bill, and at the same time keep the Conciliation Bill alive. They had enormous grass-roots support, with new branches opening in towns and villages across the country (growing in that year from 211 to 365 branches). However, despite their hard work, the Conciliation Bill's second reading, which had been passed by such a huge majority the year before, was defeated by 14 votes. Some said this was because the militant strategy of the WSPU had antagonised MPs.

However much the leaders of the national suffrage organisations might accuse and counter-accuse each other of ineffective tactics, local activity changed little – holding meetings and events aimed at winning more people over to the cause. In the following months, several meetings were arranged by the Ipswich organisations, where national speakers came to the town to lecture.

A Women's Festival of Work was planned to take place in Felixstowe over a few days in May 1912.[3] Grace Roe, Ipswich WSPU's consummate organiser, not only took a stall there, but persuaded them to give over one of their days to suffrage issues (for a fair balance, the organisers gave some time to anti-suffrage speakers on another day). The festival was opened on 8 May by Lady Beatrice Pretyman, whose husband was the local MP, and there were stalls by the National Union of Women Workers, the Salvation and Church Armies,

*Lady Geraldine's Speech* by Beatrice Harraden was an extremely popular and often-performed suffrage propaganda play. Dr Alice Romney is just about to hold a suffrage meeting at her house when her old school friend Lady Geraldine arrives unexpectedly. Lady Geraldine wants help from Alice in writing a speech she is to give at an anti-suffrage meeting and Alice, who does not like to admit that she is actually a suffragette, begins to help her. Just then, her four suffragette friends arrive – an artist, a professor of literature, a musician and a typist – who all talk so passionately about their work and about suffrage that Lady Geraldine is converted. It was an appropriate play to put on at a Women's Festival of Work.

the suffrage and anti-suffrage organisations and craftswomen. Women were in charge of all these stalls and ran demonstrations of crafts, metalwork and dairy skills as well as putting on various entertainment. On the whole, it was a festival about women's emerging role in the world.

The next day was much more political. Lady Isabel Margesson, a suffragette from London, spoke about how, once women got the vote, something could be done about sweated labour – 99 per cent of which was done by women. There were the highly political entertainments at which the suffragettes excelled, and the Actresses' Franchise League sent actresses to support the efforts of local women. Miss Sydney Keith recited Laurence Housman's *Women This and Women That*, a satire on men's conventional attitudes towards women, as well as three other recitations. In the evening the play *Lady Geraldine's Speech* was performed by seven local women including Jane Steward, Miss Douglas Reid, Mrs B.S. King and Miss Bishop. Finally, Lady Stout, a suffragette from New Zealand, spoke about what women had achieved in that country since they had the vote.

For some reason, it had not proved easy to form a suffrage group in Felixstowe. Constance Andrews had tried to do so, and certainly she had a handful of committed WFL members there. Grace Roe, however, did manage to mobilise women for the festival with the support of a newcomer to the town, Ethel Lowy. Ethel was a member of a London Jewish family, all of whom favoured suffrage for women. Her mother was a committed suffragette who had been to prison more than once for street demonstrations and breaking windows. Ethel was the oldest of four sisters, and at least two others were also active in the WSPU. She may have come to live in Felixstowe for personal reasons, or to support Grace Roe in the East Anglian campaign. In February 1912 she became local secretary, and a small group met regularly to prepare the material for the festival. Their stall would have included books, pamphlets, the national suffrage magazine *Votes for Women*, and fundraising items, and would have been lavishly decorated in purple, white and green. Ipswich suffragette, Margaret Fison, contributed a poster-sized cartoon of an ostrich with his head in the sand, called 'Anti-Suffrage Ostrich'. In the run-up to the festival there were publicity campaigns in nearby villages. Grace Roe hoped to open a shop in Felixstowe to build on the success of the festival, but there is no evidence that this happened, or that the Felixstowe group continued as an entity in its own right.

The WSPU always loved big events, and now Grace Roe came up with the most ambitious so far in this area – she gained permission to have a demonstration in Alexandra Park in July 1912. Unfortunately, none of the press reports give the numbers that attended, but all suggest they were very large.[4] Following the practice of similar events in London, there were three platforms (waggons) located at different places in the park. Each platform had a chairwoman (Grace Roe, her East Anglian co-organiser Olive Bartels, and London-based Kathleen Jarvis), and two speakers (the names of four speakers are given – Georgina Black, Barbara Wylie, Miss Douglas Smith from London, and Margaret West, the WSPU organiser in Norfolk fresh from a successful by-election campaign). In view of what was happening in the national campaign, it's not surprising that the speakers sought to justify the recent militant window smashing, referring to how men had felt forced to resort to violence in their fight for the vote years ago. They also spoke of the forty years of protest that had already passed with no result, and the thirty bills in parliament which had received a majority in favour of giving women the vote, but with no outcome. There was a group of about a hundred 'hooligans' who went round with their bugles, heckling. According to an *East Anglian Daily Times* reporter, 'they did not get the best of it', suggesting big, supportive crowds. At the end of each session a motion was put forward:

> That this great meeting in Alexandra Park protests against the non-inclusion of women in the Franchise Bill now before Parliament. It calls on the Government to put an end to the militant campaign by … carrying through all its stages in the House of Commons this session, a real reform granting the vote to men and women on equal terms.[5]

The press mentions that 'great credit must go to Grace Roe for all the arrangements which were admirable and successful'. We can only imagine what these
might have been – posters, banners, leaflets, magazines; the women would have
been dressed in the WSPU colours, and the waggons beautifully decorated.

Meanwhile, the local WFL group may have lacked some impetus without
Constance Andrews, but they continued with their meetings, selling their
newspaper, *The Vote*, and holding events.

Hortense Lane and Dr Elizabeth Knight again created maximum publicity
for the issue of taxation without representation when their seized goods were
once more auctioned at Woodbridge. Even the *East Anglian Daily Times* found
it amusing:

> Dr Knight and Hortense Lane made their annual protest against the taxa-
> tion of voteless women yesterday when their waggon was sold by auction
> ... if a waggon could only speak, it would have quite an experience to relate
> for this is the third time it has been the pivot around which these two deter-
> mined suffragettes make their protest ... Several local suffragettes were
> there – Constance Andrews, (the first lady in Great Britain to go to prison
> for tax evasion) and Grace Roe ... The waggon was sold and returned to the
> women by a private buyer. There was no heckling and some farmers were
> obviously impressed.[6]

In December 1912, Isobel Tippett joined the growing number of local suffragettes prosecuted for tax evasion. She too refused to buy a dog licence, and
appeared at Stow Petty Sessions on 2 December. The *Stowmarket Weekly Post*
of that week described her as a 'well-known novelist and advocate of women's
suffrage'. She apparently drove to court in her motor car with a large banner
proclaiming: 'Taxation Without Representation is Tyranny'. She was fined
ten shillings but announced to the court that she would not pay and had
signed over her possessions so no goods could be taken in lieu. No record has
been found as to the final outcome.

In the early summer of 1912 the WFL opened their own shop at No. 22
Queen Street, Ipswich, 'thanks to the generosity of Mrs Tippett and others'.
Now Ipswich had two shops dedicated to suffrage issues – the WSPU shop
in Dial Lane with Evelyn King in charge, and this new one just a couple of
minutes' walk away in Queens Street. When Constance Andrews saw it, she
described it as such:

A pretty little shop everyone calls it with its windows draped with hangings of green, white and gold; forming a frame for literature and posters. An array of dolls testifies to the energy of the Woolpit group who sent them for sale, and articles of various descriptions attract passers by. Go inside and find tea, cakes and other good things. A room at the back is a meeting room for WFL ... It is open 10–7pm. Thanks also to Mrs McCrery, Miss Brett and Miss Bobby.[7]

The street directory of that time shows that No. 22 Queen Street was in fact a confectionary run by Miss Bobby.[8] She had become a suffragette, and was involved in many WFL meetings and events.

Constance Andrews and the WFL campaigning caravan, which had already wended its way through Hertfordshire and Essex, arrived in Ipswich early in August. As was the usual practice, the suffragettes stopped in the town centre to hold a meeting and give out literature. There was also a get-together at Lilla Pratt's house in Norwich Road. After a few days, the caravan moved north through Suffolk and into Norfolk with both Constance and Charlotte Despard on board.

Constance Andrews seems to have been on the caravan almost constantly that summer. She and her colleagues experienced the exhilaration of 'being in charge', the unaccustomed feelings of responsibility, achievement and empowerment. It was seen as an important, highly valued aspect of the political work. As Charlotte Despard said, 'It should be remembered that through our caravan we are able to touch places that can't be touched in any other way.'[9] There must have been women hearing for the first time about what it could mean to have the vote, and responding positively.

However, the summer of 1912 was extremely wet. Again and again the two women refer to the rain in their reports in *The Vote*, and how it affected their ability to give out literature and hold open-air meetings. Then there were always opponents and hecklers. When they were in Haverhill, for example, Constance reported that a group of youths prevented them from having a public meeting, and also damaged the caravan so it had to have costly repairs. In addition, these youths surrounded their lodgings during the night, making so much noise they could not sleep.[10] Through these stories, we see how committed Constance Andrews continued to be, facing new situations daily with courage and determination.

# Stalemate

The year ended badly for the WSPU, which was experiencing a difficult time with most of its leaders in prison and Christabel Pankhurst abroad. There was a breakdown in the long-established leadership. The window-breaking campaign had lost the cause a lot of support, and Mr and Mrs Pethwick-Lawrence wanted to mount a major educational initiative to explain it, and help people accept it. Emmeline Pankhurst and Christabel disagreed, and suddenly without warning they dismissed the Pethwick-Lawrences. The shock was felt throughout the suffrage world. They had been an exceptionally close group, and the Pethwick-Lawrences had bankrolled the WSPU and pretty much bankrupted themselves in the name of the cause. Now Emmeline and Christabel alone led the WSPU into a new, yet more militant phase.

A difference in the language used was immediately apparent when Emmeline Pankhurst visited Ipswich on 12 February 1913. Gone was the cheerful optimism shown by national leaders only a few months previously. Now the talk was of war. The WSPU, in shedding so many of its leaders, had lost its diversity of opinion about how best to conduct the campaign. Now there was just the authoritarian, militant two-person leadership of Christabel and Emmeline Pankhurst. Moreover, the Liberal government was still, after all these years, finding ways to thwart the women's demands.

On 23 January 1913, cabinet ministers Lloyd George and Edward Grey had received a deputation of 300 working women drawn from across the country. Twenty of these were selected to speak, reminding the ministers of the contribution women made to the country through their work, and delineating the reasons why they should have the vote. The ministers received the words of these women in a positive way. However, the very same day, the Speaker of the House of Commons announced that the amendments submitted for inclusion in the Reform Bill would change it too much, and a new Conciliation Bill would have to be drafted. Effectively, this killed off all current attempts to get legislation giving women the vote through parliament.

All of the suffrage societies were enraged, with even the moderate NUWSS feeling betrayed, so perhaps Mrs Pankhurst's language was not so surprising when she addressed the meeting at Ipswich's Co-operative Hall just a couple of weeks later. Whereas before she had approved 'the argument of the stone' and attacks on property, now her language was of war.[11] Her point was that there were several wars across the world in which people were killing others in defence of their beliefs, and this seemed acceptable to the government, if regrettable.

The same judgement should be applied to women, who, although declaring war to achieve their aims, were not aiming to take anyone's life. In the absence of this understanding, the targets would be any property belonging to establishment figures and the state, until the vote was won.

For those who remained loyal to the WSPU and the tactics of the Pankhursts, there began to play out an intense struggle between women activists and the state. Dozens of empty buildings were burnt – often at night so the perpetrators were seldom caught – and golf courses had slogans cut into the turf such as 'No Vote, No Golf'. The one rule was that no one must be injured or threatened in these actions. The aim was to show that it was impossible to govern without the consent of the governed.

Where women were caught and prosecuted, they hunger struck in prison, and with forcible feeding often had to be discharged early on health grounds. In April 1913 the government passed the Prisoners' Temporary Discharge for Ill-health Act. Immediately dubbed 'The Cat and Mouse Act', its intent was that women would be released from prison on licence whenever they became weak and ill from hunger striking, but must be returned as soon as their health improved. Some women made the most of the cat and mouse aspect of this, refusing to return to prison on licence and engaging with the authorities in long games of hide and seek, using disguises, and appearing triumphantly on the platforms of public meetings. But some women, including Emmeline Pankhurst, now in her mid-50s, and her daughter Sylvia, became emaciated and so weak that they had to be carried on stretchers or bath chairs. Any 'recovery' was quickly lost as soon as they returned to prison. Emmeline Pankhurst, who was serving a three-year sentence for inciting others to damage property, began to feel that the stalemate between the state and the suffragettes could only be broken by martyrdom. Her death appeared to be just a matter of time.

However, it was another woman who became the martyr. On 4 June 1913, Emily Wilding Davison, a long-term committed militant suffragette, tried to pin a Votes for Women sash to the king's horse at the Epsom Derby during the race. She was thrown through the air by the horse's hoofs, and her injuries were so severe that she died four days later. There was an enormous outpouring of grief for her, and a huge procession in London was carefully choreographed to achieve maximum effect before she was taken to her home town of Morpeth, where she was buried.

During these months, while Christabel Pankhurst was co-ordinating events as best she could from Paris, and Emmeline and other trusted leaders were in prison or weak from hunger striking, Grace Roe became the effective organ-iser of the campaign in this country. She had already been drawn away from Ipswich during the previous year, though she still managed to organise some local events like the Alexandra Park demonstration. But now she focused on putting into effect the orders of Christabel. At the same time, she was under continuous threat of arrest herself, and had to go about in disguise, always arranging decoys and false trails to divert the police. It was she, helped by Felixstowe's Edith Lowy, who organised Emily Davison's funeral and many other events at this time. She was arrested soon afterwards for conspiracy.

Although the WFL did not agree with the nature of WSPU militancy after 1912, and certainly did not consider themselves at war with anyone, they nev-ertheless shared the same aims and supported the WSPU where they could. The WSPU were banned from most meeting halls and parks in London, but the WFL continued to hold events in these venues, and frequently the flags, ban-ners and personalities of the sister movements were seen together. Throughout the country, women continued to refuse to pay taxes, making speeches in court when prosecuted and holding public meetings.

Constance Andrews served another year on the National Executive of the WFL, increasing her skills and experience. In March 1913, she led the suffra-gettes at the by-election campaign at Houghton-le-Spring, and later in the year went to support and develop local branches in the Midlands. It is possible she was based in London during this period, returning to Ipswich between times.

However, she did attend the 1913 episode of tax evasion by persistent offenders, Hortense Lane and Dr Elizabeth Knight. At the hearing for not having a dog licence, Constance asked to appear for Dr Knight, who was unable to attend. Despite the court preferring a solicitor, she insisted, and made the point that whilst Dr Knight was professionally able to declare a man insane, and thus deprive him of the vote, she was not able to vote herself, despite paying taxes and rates.[12]

Constance also attended occasional branch meetings as a speaker in Ipswich and Hadleigh. During this year Mrs Hossack, who had been campaigning for the vote continuously for at least six years, became the Ipswich branch secretary. The shop in Queen Street remained an ongoing concern, but there were perhaps fewer significant campaigning events in Ipswich during this year than there had been for several years. The local WFL and WSPU must have felt keenly the loss of Constance Andrews and Grace Roe to the national campaigns – both equally passionate if very different women, with rare organising skills and commitment.

In June 1913, the National Union of Women's Suffrage Societies (NUWSS) organised a countrywide pilgrimage. Although this organisation always acted within the law, its members also felt furious and betrayed by a government which continued to deny women the opportunity to vote and, although their methods were very different from the WSPU and the WFL, their passionate belief that women should have the vote was exactly the same. Their organisation was growing rapidly (in 1913 they had 450 branches nationwide), and they wanted to tell women that there were alternatives to the militancy of which the newspapers were full. Women walked from various points in the country, coming together a week later in London for a weekend of rallies and demonstrations. Thousands joined the pilgrimage for some or all of the way, and the enormous, final procession in London was important in reminding the government and others that it was not just the militants who wanted the vote.

One strand of the pilgrimage came down the East Coast from Great Yarmouth via Lowestoft and Southwold, and arrived in Wickham Market on 15 June 1913. At this stage there were only a handful of 'pilgrims' intending to do the full journey, some walking and some on bicycles. As they went they gave out leaflets and held village meetings. At each stop they were greeted by local suffragists, and hosted by them. In Wickham Market, an 'at home' was hosted by Lady Mary Cayley, president of the Woodbridge branch of the NUWSS.[13] Speeches were given by national and local suffragists, and whilst they always made the point that they did not support the methods of the WSPU, their speeches were very similar – talking about the opportunities suffrage would bring to right some of the wrongs that women suffered.

The next day they moved on to Woodbridge, holding meetings at Upper and Lower Orford and Melton on the way. A local reporter writes with a slightly incredulous tone that 'there were ladies marching in procession with their banners through the Thoroughfare, watched by numerous spectators'.[14] In the evening, they held an open-air meeting on the Market Hill, where more than 700 people came to listen to their speeches.

On to Ipswich the next day; and the 'pilgrims' were met at the beginning of the Old Woodbridge Road by the members of the Ipswich and County Women's Suffrage Society (they had never affiliated themselves to the NUWSS, but were broadly in line with their approach). Some of the names mentioned in the newspaper report[15] are familiar – Miss M. Griffin, Miss Place, Miss Gardiner (honorary secretary), Mrs W.T. Griffiths, Mrs de Candole and Miss Harrison. The flag of the local group read: 'Ipswich and County WSS – A union of hearts in the service of all who live, and all who suffer.' They and many other supporters walked into town, where they had tea at the Co-operative Hall followed by open-air meetings. About twelve suffragist pilgrims left the next day for Dedham, and onwards to London.

In October 1913, the Ipswich and County Women's Suffrage Society invited the Actresses' Franchise League (AFL) to return to Ipswich and perform at the exhibition of Art in the Home and the Women's Sphere. This exhibition went on for several days at the public hall in Tavern Street, with a different theme on each day – for example, home furnishings or healthy eating. On 3 October, women's suffrage was the theme of the day, and members of the AFL came and performed a one-act play called *Mr Wilkinson's Widow*. This was reported to be:

> A very uncompromising attack on traditional relationships between men and women. The story is that strong woman Mrs Wilkinson keeps a hotel for her husband, and builds up a very successful business. On her husband's death, she has all kinds of ideas about her future, only to find that all the wealth has been left to their son, who will 'look after her for the rest of her life'. In a fit of fierce independence of spirit, she throws off her widow's weeds and goes off to spend the night at the theatre.[16]

The play was accompanied by dancing and also speeches – one of which was about women's sweated labour and how this and many other issues could be resolved if women had the vote.

During February 1914, the local Women's Freedom League held another Green, Gold and White Fair at St Lawrence's Hall in Ipswich. Again it was a mixture of propaganda stalls and fundraising. In a speech, Mrs Hossack explained that although the WFL did not go in for violence, they did not criticise those who did – there was room for all, and words had proved to be not enough.[17] They also performed a sketch entitled *The Lunatic* with local women taking the roles. Isabel Tippett, who by now was also doing suffrage campaigning at a national level, came to speak in the evening. She then led a successful campaign amongst several villages around Ipswich.

The WSPU likewise continued their local campaigning. During March 1914, a woman stood up at the end of the first act of a play being performed at the Lyceum and denounced the forcible feeding that was decimating the WSPU leadership, and showered leaflets on all of those below. *The Suffragette* reported that the speech was 'well received, the few hisses drowned out by applause'.[18]

Dr Knight and Hortense Lane had their annual tangle with the tax authorities, and once more the waggon was brought into service to be sold at auction to pay their unpaid fines, and was bought back for them by a well-wisher. Dr Knight was also under threat for refusing to pay National Insurance on her medical work in London, and went to prison for this later in the year.

Constance Andrews served another term of imprisonment in London in a different cause. The WFL, which always concerned itself with broader women's issues, had started to protest against some police officers who had allegedly lied in court to protect a colleague – a man who was suspected of having raped the 14-year-old daughter of his landlady. The WFL protested to the Home Secretary about this, and when they got no reply, started to picket the offices of the director of public prosecutions. Constance Andrews was one of twelve women who were arrested for standing outside his office with placards.[19] Fined in court for obstruction, they all refused to pay and were imprisoned in Holloway. These women were much feted on their release – a great deal was made of the fact that men get off scot-free, even after rape, when they protected each other by lying in court, but women are imprisoned just for protesting. They were given a prison badge at a large reception. In the middle of April, Constance Andrews returned to Ipswich briefly to tell her colleagues about it.

# 7

# A FINAL, LOCAL MILITANT ACT

## The burning of the Bath Hotel

If the citizens of the Ipswich area thought they had escaped the worst of the attacks on property that had become so prevalent in other parts of the country, then they were to receive a shock. Suffolk had so far been ignored in a campaign in which it seemed that no structure could be considered safe – warehouses, theatres, football stands, stations, big houses, schools, golf courses and post boxes were all deemed suitable targets. In the spring of 1914, however, arson came to the coast.

In the middle of April, the Women Teachers' Conference was held in Lowestoft. The suffrage movement felt that women's professions could only truly develop when women had the vote and equal representation in parliament, and so all the large organisations, from the least to the most militant, planned a large presence in the town to coincide with the conference. There were indoor and outdoor meetings with prominent speakers, propaganda meetings at nearby villages and towns, and acts that were considered disruptive – for example, women standing up in church to pray for suffrage, which often resulted in a hasty and sometimes brutal eviction by the stewards.

During the night of 18 April 1914, in the middle of the conference weekend, the pavilion on the pier at Great Yarmouth was burnt down, and the pier itself damaged, causing thousands of pounds worth of damage right at the start of the holiday season. Suffragette messages were found on the beach nearby. No one was ever charged with this offence (fire-setting suffragettes were often not discovered because their acts took place at night), but later it was thought likely to have been done by Hilda Birkett and Florence Tunks, two militant Women's Social and Political Union (WSPU) suffragettes who were staying near Lowestoft during the conference. They then came to stay at No. 32 Berners Street, Ipswich on the 19 April.

**HILDA BIRKETT** (1876–1955) was a long-term militant suffragette, and at this time was a 'Mouse' – that is, she was on licence from prison. She had been convicted at the end of 1913 for setting fire to stands at Leeds football ground, and after a period of hunger striking and forcible feeding, had been released under the 'Cat and Mouse Act'. She was given a period of time to recover from the effects on her health of her treatment in prison, and then was expected to return to continue her sentence. Like many such suffragettes, she was avoiding this by moving around the country.

She was a very committed suffragette who had joined the WSPU in 1907, and become the organiser of the Birmingham branch. In 1909, when Prime Minister Asquith came to Birmingham to give a speech to an audience of 10,000 people, she succeeded, with others, in throwing stones at his special railway carriage. She was arrested and given one month in prison, where she started to hunger strike. This group of women were the first in the country to be forcibly fed. She could have had no idea what was going to happen to her when, already weak and ill from lack of food, she was dragged into a room where she was held down whilst a tube was stuck down her throat into her stomach. She experienced this again in 1912 and 1913 – like many suffragettes the daily torture of forcible feeding only served to strengthen her purpose.

On the other hand her companion at Felixstowe, Florence Tunks, was a relative novice. She was a young woman from South Wales, and these seem to have been her first militant activities.

The movements of the two women were pieced together by the police with the help of a diary that they confiscated and used as evidence in court.[1] The brief record of 22 and 23 April shows that they stayed in Ipswich but found it 'very disappointing' and 'all disappointments'. This could refer to a lack of support from suffragette contacts (Grace Roe was organising in London at this time), or perhaps that security in the town made arson attacks difficult.

On 24 April, the two women went out on bikes for the day from their Ipswich lodgings – they would have appeared to be holidaymakers to anyone observing them – and cycled out in the general direction of Felixstowe through Nacton and Levington. Just north of Trimley, on Bucklesham Farm, which was owned by local MP Mr Pretyman, they set fire to two stacks of wheat. They left luggage labels tied to the nearby hedge which said 'Votes for Women' on one side, and 'Asquith is responsible, apply to him for damages' on the other. A copy of *The Suffragette* newspaper was also left open at a page about a woman in prison who had been forcibly fed for fourteen weeks.

The next day, a 'stover' (cornstalk) stack went up in flames at nearby Stratton Hall, a farm owned by a Mr Dawson. It was thought an incendiary device left by the women the day before may have been triggered by the heat of the day. The two women had been spotted near the farm, though it was only when they were arrested in Felixstowe a few days later that any suspicion as regards these fires was attached to them. The day after Mr Pretyman's stacks were burnt, Hilda Birkett and Florence Tunks booked into a guesthouse in Felixstowe for a week.

It is a matter of speculation as to whether, on their arrival in Felixstowe, Hilda Birkett and Florence Tunks met with local suffragettes to discuss the action they were intending to take. There were local members of the Women's Freedom League in the town, who had been part of the Ipswich group's activities over many years, but their organisation did not support the arson campaign. The WSPU had recruited several members in the town, especially after 1912 when Edith Lowy moved to Felixstowe to assist Grace Roe there. It is possible that Hilda Birkett and Florence Tunks met with Edith Lowy to discuss possible targets.

On the weekend of 25 April 1914, there were rumours, or fears, in Felixstowe that there might be an arson attack. These concerns would have stemmed from the Great Yarmouth fire and the farm fires nearby, and night-watchmen were employed to guard the pier and the Spa Pavilion. Whether either of these was an original target for the two suffragettes, we do not know. Many of the decisions about targets generally appear to have been quite arbitrary.

Until the beginning of the century, the Bath Hotel was the finest in the town. It was in fact the first hotel to be built there, in 1839, and was originally known as the Hamilton Arms. The name was changed in 1867 when baths were put in. For thirty years after that, it was thought of as a 'millionaires' retreat', due to its position just above the beach and the facilities it provided – bathing machines, hot and cold seawater baths, sporting facilities and its proximity to the Golf Club. It was a fairly large establishment and had fifty-five bedrooms. Despite the building, in 1903, of the larger and smarter Felix Hotel just up the road, it was still a favourite with people like Lord Balfour (a vocal opponent of women's suffrage, although his sister was a leading supporter), and with wealthy people wanting a few days' escape from London.

The Bath Hotel was not open on this weekend at the end of April. It was being refurbished ready for the imminent start of the holiday season. Perhaps Edith Lowy was able to tell Hilda Birkett and Florence Tunks this when they were selecting their target. It was a matter of policy in the WSPU that whatever damage was done to property, human life was not to be threatened.

The two women hired a beach tent near the pier, and acted in a way that gave their landlady no suspicion that they were anything but two young women enjoying a holiday at the seaside. On Monday, 27 April, they told her that they were going to the theatre in Ipswich that evening, and would stay overnight with a friend as there was no transport back. In fact, they stayed in Felixstowe and were observed leaving their beach tent early in the evening.[2] At around 10 p.m. they were out and about in the vicinity of the Bath Hotel, where they were spotted by a Commander White.

There were still a few hours to go before the fire was started. They must have continued for a while to walk around the beach area, as they were observed near the pier at about 1 a.m. In addition, there were preparations to make. They broke a window in the hotel's kitchen, and used soft soap to stick cotton wool to the edges of the broken glass to protect their hands. Then they were able to unlatch the window, open it and get in. They chose a site for the fire deep inside the hotel, and set their incendiary materials. They also had labels to prepare and fix to nearby trees. These labels said: 'There can be no peace until women get the vote', and 'No Vote means War, Votes for Women means Peace'.

The fire was noticed at about 4 a.m., and firefighters and police were soon on the scene. A large crowd gathered, and Hilda Birkett and Florence Tunks were seen there laughing and joking about the fire. By about 9 a.m., the hotel was completely burnt out – one of the problems being that the local fire service was not equipped to tackle such a large fire, and there was insufficient water available to put it out.

The next morning, the two women returned to their guesthouse pretending to have arrived back at Felixstowe from Ipswich. They were arrested later that day and remanded in custody at Ipswich Gaol. There was some suggestion that procedure was not followed – there was no warrant for the police to enter their room and arrest them or search their possessions; Felixstowe police station acted as an 'occasional court', and remanded the women without granting them access to lawyers.

## Forcible feeding in Ipswich

Following the fire and the arrests, there was deep unrest in both Felixstowe and Ipswich. Feelings ran high against these two women and suffragettes in general, and people did not hesitate to show their hostility. At the same time local suffragettes, many of whom may not have approved of the arson action, were determined to support Hilda Birkett and Florence Tunks and use their situation as publicity for their campaign. A further ingredient in this potent mix was an Ipswich by-election. The Liberal MP Sylvester Horne had tragically and unexpectedly died, and polling day was set for 23 May 1914.

On 2 May, suffrage supporters held a meeting of support outside the prison in Grimwade Street where the two women were being held on remand.[3] There was a large hostile crowd, and the police would not allow the suffragettes to speak. On another day, they held a meeting at the end of Orchard Street facing the prison's main gates. Apparently, the crowd set upon the speaker causing her to fall, and 'tore off her hat and other portions of clothing, flaunting them as trophies'. The suffrage paper reported that Hilda Birkett and Florence Tunks were hunger striking and being forcibly fed, despite never being convicted. The WSPU shop, now situated at No. 6 Tower Street, Ipswich, covered its windows with posters decrying this. *The Suffragette*, in its newspaper dated 15 May, reported that the hoardings were 'causing particular comment, and much sympathy is being expressed. One woman was heard to exclaim "How terrible it is. I had no idea force feeding was like that".'

On 6 May, the suffrage stall at the annual Felixstowe Exhibition at the Spa Pavilion was not allowed to stand. Originally, the intention had been for all the local suffrage societies to have a stall there, but the more militant organisations withdrew to focus their resources on the issues surrounding the women in Ipswich Gaol and the impending by-election. However, the non-militant National Union of Women's Suffrage Societies (NUWSS), which would have utterly condemned the burning of the hotel, decided to go ahead. The Felixstowe NUWSS was organised by Edith Place of Quilter Road, and ironically its president was Mr Cowles, head of the Fire Service, who had so recently led the fight against the fire at the Bath Hotel. Some young men were unable to see the subtle differences between the organisations and trashed the stall.[4] The police were called and a free fight ensued which was only ended when a fire hose was turned on them. The goods on

the stall were thrown into the sea by excited onlookers, and the exhibition had to be closed for the day.

When Hilda Birkett and Florence Tunks appeared at the magistrates' court in Felixstowe on 15 May, a journalist said that there was little sign of them having been forcibly fed.[5] However, Hilda Birkett was said to be faint when she got out of the carriage to go into court, and was reported at times to seem exhausted. A large, mainly hostile, crowd met their carriage when it arrived at the court on the seafront, and remained there throughout the proceedings. When the women came out of court, a supporting suffragette was thrown into the horse trough at the bottom of Bent Hill.

The evidence was heard over two days and the two women were remanded to Bury Assizes charged with setting fire to the stacks of Mr Dawson and Mr Pretyman, and of burning down the Bath Hotel. Charges relating to the fire on Great Yarmouth pier were dropped.

Throughout the proceedings, Hilda Birkett and Florence Tunks kept up a defiant attitude. They would not confirm their names, and sat throughout on a table with their backs to the magistrate. They chatted and laughed whilst evidence was given, and refused to challenge the accounts of others, or give any themselves. They only reacted when Commander White of the Royal Navy, gave evidence that he had seen them near the Bath Hotel on that evening. When he gave his evidence at each of the trials, the two women exploded in anger. According to the press report:

> When Commander White came into the witness box the two women threw their shoes at him and shouted loud verbal abuse. They tried to reach him. There was a long struggle to quieten them down. They accused the Commander of trying to seduce them.[6]

When they were remanded in custody again, *The Suffragette*, on 22 May, reported Hilda Birkett as saying: 'I defy Mr McKenna (the Home Secretary) to keep me in prison as long as he wishes, torture me as he may, for I shall get out some time, alive or dead.'

The presence in Ipswich Gaol of two hunger-striking women who were being forcibly fed whilst awaiting trial formed the backdrop to the by-election campaign. By-elections were traditional battlegrounds for the suffrage groups. They used them as an opportunity to talk to local people about the facts of who was allowed to vote and who was not, and what the position of the candidates was on this single issue. In recent years, they had turned out not so much to support any suffrage-minded candidate as to oppose the Liberal government, urging others not to vote for Liberal candidates who, whatever their personal views, would become part of a system that was systematically denying half the population the vote. In Ipswich, they also used the opportunity to talk about the two women in its prison – women who were normally law-abiding but who felt so strongly about votes for women that they were prepared to commit arson to achieve it, and undergo the horrors of hunger striking and forcible feeding.

Both the WSPU and the Women's Freedom League (WFL) sent national organisers to Ipswich to conduct the by-election campaign. Numerous meetings were held in the town, both indoors and out. Many people felt shocked that in their own town, doctors and wardresses were pinning down women who had not yet been convicted and forcing food down their throats. For example, a deputation of townspeople to the Bishop of Ipswich heard him express his complete disagreement and horror at what was happening. At the same time, the Church was determined not to allow suffrage protest. Women who got up during services at St Margaret's and Tacket Street churches and prayed for the health of the forcibly fed women were evicted from the service by stewards.[7]

The suffragettes in Ipswich had a stormy ride. *The Vote*, the national paper of the WFL, usually so moderate in its language, acknowledged the services of those who at Ipswich 'took their lives in their hands during a campaign of such brutal, insensate and obscene violence and indecency as has rarely been equalled and never exceeded', adding that the suffragettes 'finally won the respectful sympathy of the people whose antagonism they broke down'.[8] The campaign for votes for women in Ipswich had been accompanied by heckling throughout – during the by-election the heckling erupted into violence.

In her report in the same paper, Alice Munro said:

After a strenuous fight – victory ... to see youths and young men adorned with Liberal colours and anti-suffrage badges fighting free speech and argument by knocking women down and pelting them with missiles, hard and soft, smashing the platform, running the waggon around the town with the intention of throwing us in the river, wrenching our hats off our heads, tearing our clothes and behaving with grossest indecency. The police throughout were magnificent. Thanks to Mr and Mrs Lane who brought their waggon to prevent a repetition of the horse play. By Thursday or Friday, their pluck began to tell, and they were listened to and applauded. In spite of the precautions for Mr Lloyd George when he came to Ipswich, Mrs Hossack greeted him with a Votes for Women banner as he left by special train.

The waggon referred to was probably the famous one that had so frequently been auctioned and repurchased to repay Hortense Lane's unpaid fines.[9]

The suffrage organisations must have felt that they had a victory to claim when the Liberal candidate Mr Masterman (a cabinet member) was unexpectedly defeated, and Unionist Mr Ganzani won by a sizeable majority of 532 votes. Intense excitement was reported on polling day with thousands of people in the street. Mr Ganzani would in fact show very lukewarm support to the suffrage cause in the future.

There is no sign that Grace Roe was in town at this very turbulent time. As the national leadership of the WSPU decreased with so many key women in prison, or, if out on licence, weakened and ill and technically unable to make public appearances, Grace Roe had become leader under the absent Christabel Pankhurst's direction. However, Grace herself was arrested in London at around the same time as the Ipswich by-election. There was a sense that leadership of the WSPU was failing, that it did not have control over many of the militant acts of its members, or any real policy direction. The government saw this, and kept up the pressure of the law. Emmeline Pankhurst was still serving the sentence imposed on her in 1912 – she was never forcibly fed, but released on licence again and again as she became weak from hunger striking. Although when out on licence, she would still use disguise and make miraculous appearances at the most important public meetings, she was becoming emaciated and weak.

In March 1914, well-known militant suffragette Mary Richardson entered the National Gallery and slashed the famous painting, *The Rokeby Venus* by Velazquez. This was controversial even amongst supporters. In her defence, she wrote:

I have tried to destroy the most beautiful woman in mythological history as a protest against the Government destroying Mrs Pankhurst, who is the most beautiful character in modern history. If there is an outcry against my deed, let everyone remember that such an outcry is an hypocrisy as long as they allow the destruction of Mrs Pankhurst and other beautiful living women.[10]

The result of this action was to close the National Gallery and The Tate. Other galleries remained open, but for a time women were only allowed to enter if accompanied by a man or if they had a letter of recommendation.

These worries were reflected around the country. The curator of the Borough of Ipswich Museum wrote to a colleague on 23 June 1914:

> At the time of the late election here we know a lot of these objectionable creatures were down from London and staying in the town. We therefore put a night watchman in ... The value of collections cannot be estimated. They could never be replaced if once destroyed ... The police here are our most loyal allies, and I am a frequent visitor at the Police Station with any suspicious information I come across.[11]

A week after the by-election, the arson case against Hilda Birkett and Florence Tunks was heard at Bury Assizes. The two women continued their disruptive behaviour in court, refusing to plead, and objecting to the all-male jury. They chatted and laughed throughout, and once again Commander White received the full force of their fury and derision. Hilda Birkett said, 'He thought we were girls he could seduce. You only believe such men as Commandeer White, curse him.'

When it came to their final statements, the local newspaper reports Hilda Birkett saying:

> ... that justice could not be given to women in that court, because it was composed entirely of men. Neither could she be expected to state her case properly, because she had been in prison nearly five weeks, during which time she had been forcibly fed and tortured ... In her solitary confinement she had no privileges, she had no books, papers, and no exercise ... she went on to say that a great deal of fuss was being made about a bit of property being destroyed, but women were risking their lives and liberty in order to bring the wrongs of their sex to the notice of the world.[12]

She was stopped from telling the court of the attempts women had made for over forty years to get the vote. Florence Tunks merely said how proud she was to be standing with her friend in court that day.

Hilda Birkett was sentenced to two years' imprisonment. Florence Tunks received a sentence of nine months, as according to the judge, she was a 'tool of others', and had no previous convictions. They were returned to Ipswich Gaol and transferred to Holloway on 1 June.

A few days later, the Ipswich WSPU held a public meeting at the Co-operative Hall to discuss forcible feeding. A Dr Moxon from London spoke, and stated that he did not have a political view about votes for women, but his opposition to forcible feeding was made on medical and ethical grounds.[13] No one resisting food should be forcibly fed against their will, and if they were, it had to be an individual medical decision made for the benefit of the individual patient. He felt it was quite wrong for doctors to collaborate with the government in this way. He also spoke about the fact that doctors in prison were now giving drugs to women to quieten their resistance, and urged the people of Ipswich to laud Grace Roe, who had recently appeared in court in an obviously drugged state.[14]

The reference is to her appearance at Marylebone magistrates' court on 29 May 1914 on charges of conspiracy, when Grace Roe was seen to try to behave in her usual spirited, resistant way, but seemed drowsy and exhausted. 'I have been drugged,' she said. 'They are drugging women in prison because they know that however much we are tortured, we shall never give in.'[15] On 8 July, she was sentenced to three months in prison.

Over the next few months, Hilda Birkett and Florence Tunks experienced a difficult time in gaol, as did Grace Roe. When Mary Richardson, also in Holloway for damaging *The Rokeby Venus*, was released under the Cat and Mouse Act in August 1914, she gave a report on each of the dozen or so suffragette prisoners in Holloway.[16] She said that Grace Roe was in solitary confinement and was being forcibly fed three times daily. She was extremely thin and in pain, with a cut mouth and bruised ankles.

Of Hilda Birkett she said, 'She suffers agonies with her nerves. She is quite alone and is forcibly fed four times daily. She is sick after every feeding and has lost over a stone. Her throat is in a terrible condition. She has been forcibly fed over 250 times.'

Of Florence Tunks she said, 'She has lost 2 stone and 4 pounds. She has got broken teeth from the gags and has hurt her nose a lot. She is in a nervous condition, and cannot stand for faintness.'

Such reports are a reminder of the brutality of forcible feeding, and the daily agony suffered by the women. It raises the question of whether they needed to be fed so many times a day, and whether this excess, in conjunction with the methods used, bordered on torture.

Grace Roe, Hilda Birkett and Florence Tunks did not have to survive their full sentences. When war was declared in August 1914, all of the suffragettes were released from prison under an amnesty, and this proved to be the end of the campaign. When Florence Tunks' family came to meet her at the prison gates, they were shocked and declared that, 'she was virtually unrecognisable ... a skeleton'.[17] For some reason, Hilda Birkitt was not released until 1 September, making her both one of the first and one of the last suffragettes to be forcibly fed.

*Clockwise from top left*
1  Elizabeth Garrett Anderson about 1865 – instigator of the Ladies'
Petition 1866. (Garrett Family Album)
2  Matilda Betham Edwards of Westerfield – signatory of the Ladies'
Petition 1866. (Author's collection)
3  '*Non angeli sed Angli*' – Mary Lowndes' East Anglia banner
(*See* page 33). (Courtesy of The Women's Library at LSE (2ASL/11/09))

4 Constance Andrews on the Trades Union Congress Reception Committee, Ipswich, 1909. (Author's collection)

5 Women's Freedom League caravan at Felixstowe, 1910 – Lilla Pratt is on the left and Constance Andrews in the middle. (Reproduced by permission of The National Library of Scotland)

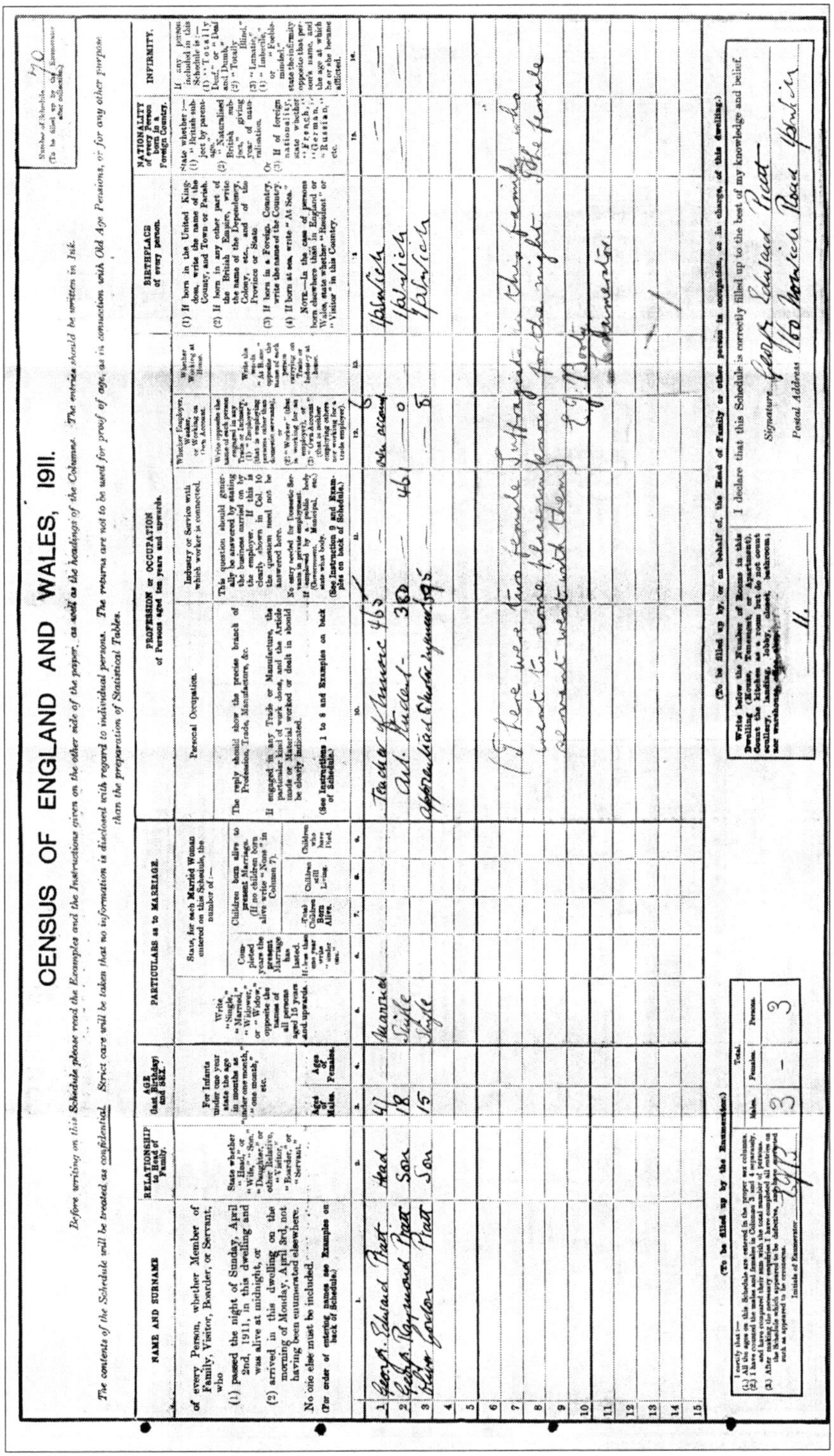

# CENSUS OF ENGLAND AND WALES, 1911.

Number of Schedule 70

*Before writing on this Schedule please read the Examples and the Instructions given on the other side of the paper, as well as the headings of the Columns. The entries should be written in Ink.*

*The contents of the Schedule will be treated as confidential. Strict care will be taken that no information is disclosed with regard to individual persons. The returns are not to be used for proof of age, as in connection with Old Age Pensions, or for any other purpose than the preparation of Statistical Tables.*

| | Name and Surname | Relationship to Head of Family | Age of Males | Age of Females | Particulars as to Marriage | Personal Occupation | Industry or Service | Employer, Worker, or Own Account | Birthplace | Nationality | Infirmity |
|---|---|---|---|---|---|---|---|---|---|---|---|
| 1 | George Edward Pratt | Head | 47 | | Married | Teacher of Music 465 | — | own account 6 | Ipswich | — | — |
| 2 | George Raymond Pratt | Son | 18 | | Single | Art Student 380 | — 461 | — 0 | Ipswich | | |
| 3 | Oliver Gordon Pratt | Son | 15 | | Single | apprenticed Motor engineer 595 | — | — 5 | Ipswich | | |

(There were two female Suffragists in this family who went to some place unknown for the night. The female servant went with them) E. J. Booty Enumerator.

(To be filled up by the Enumerator.) Initials of Enumerator E J B. Total: Males 3, Females –, Persons 3.

(To be filled up by, or on behalf of, the Head of Family or other person in occupation, or in charge, of this dwelling.) Number of Rooms: 11.

I declare that this Schedule is correctly filled up to the best of my knowledge and belief.

Signature George Edward Pratt

Postal Address 160 Norwich Road Ipswich

6 The 1911 census schedule of Constance Andrews' household. (Courtesy of the National Archives, London)

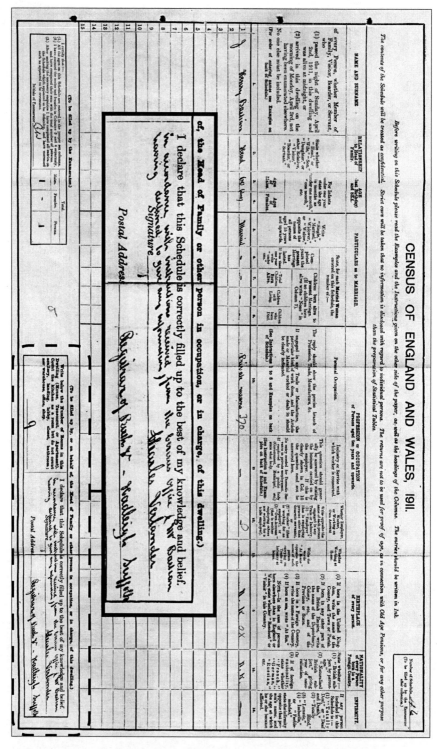

7 The 1911 census schedule of the Bastian household. Note the enumerator's comment in the signature box. (Courtesy of the National Archives, London)

8 Extract from the criminal register, Ipswich, 1908–21, showing the entry for Constance Andrews. (Courtesy of Suffolk Record Office)

9 The burning of the Bath Hotel, Felixstowe, April 1914. (Courtesy of Suffolk Record Office)

10  Constance Andrews' release from Ipswich Prison. (Courtesy of Suffolk Record Office)

11  Suffragette demonstration in Alexandra Park, Ipswich, 1912. (Courtesy of The Women's Library at LSE (TWL.2002.35))

12 The WSPU shop in Tower Street, Ipswich. (Courtesy of The Women's Library at LSE)

13 Two suffragettes arrive at Felixstowe Court, April 1914. (Courtesy of Suffolk Record Office)

# AFTERWORD

**T**HE SUFFRAGETTES CEASED their militant campaign as soon as war was declared with Germany in August 1914. Emmeline and Christabel Pankhurst immediately decided that the suffrage cause was secondary to the need to support the country, and the Ipswich Women's Social and Political Union (WSPU), like many other branches, came to an end. The Ipswich Women's Freedom League (WFL) was renamed the Women's Suffrage Aid Corps in common with similar suffrage groups. Women of all kinds threw their energy and skills into supporting the war effort and, as the war went on, became indispensable to the functioning of the country. 'Women were still campaigning [for the vote] by demonstrating exemplary citizenship.'[1]

The WSPU nationally disbanded, but the National Union of Women's Suffrage Societies and the WFL retained their organisations, although there were many splits and disputes over the direction they should take. Women's suffrage was not forgotten, and many continued to work for it in a quiet way. They were, therefore, in a good position to press the government to include some franchise of women when, in 1916, there was a need to change the regulations concerning the electoral register. The register was no longer fit for purpose with so many men serving abroad, and the government also wanted to widen the franchise to include working men – the backbone of the fighting.

The government was not able to ignore the contribution of women any more, but also wanted to avoid a situation where more women than men would have the vote. In the end, the 1918 Representation of the People Act gave the vote to all men over 21 and most women over 30. The Act was carried by 385 MPs for, and 55 against. The women over 30 who were excluded were those who lived in furnished lodgings or with family members. It was an unjust compromise, especially as it was mainly working women who remained disenfranchised, but the suffrage organisations reluctantly accepted it because the general principle was established that women should have the vote. An amendment soon afterwards allowed women to stand as parliamentary candidates. At the 1918 general election sixteen did so, of which many were prominent suffragettes, including Christabel Pankhurst and Charlotte Despard. Only the Irish Sinn Fein candidate Constance Markievicz was successful, but she chose not to take her seat, and it was only at a by-election in 1919 that Nancy Astor became the first woman to take a seat as a Member of Parliament.

At the 1923 general election, eight women became MPs out of seventeen candidates in a parliament with a minority Labour government. Again, the government refused to widen the franchise, and the old cycle of private members' bills that did not produce any outcome was repeated. In 1926 the suffrage organisations, together with many other groups seeking equality for women, held a huge procession and pressed the government through lobbying and meetings.

In 1928, under a Conservative government, the Equal Franchise Act was passed, giving the vote to all women and men over the age of 21. Emmeline Pankhurst died just days before the bill was passed in the House of Lords, knowing it was secure. In a general election the following year fourteen women were elected as MPs and one, Margaret Bondfield, became the first woman cabinet minister. Ipswich would have to wait until 1957 for Miss Manuela Sykes to stand for the Liberals as its first female parliamentary candidate, but the town still has not had a woman MP. Suffolk's first woman MP, Therese Coffey, was elected in 2010 for Suffolk Coastal.

Social movements throw up people who would otherwise be nameless, only for them to disappear from public view when circumstances change, and we do not know what happened to most of the suffragettes in the Ipswich area after the war. They may have joined other social or political reforming groups, or have been happy to continue with other aspects of their lives. We do know that Isobel Tippett and her husband travelled widely in Europe. What about Constance Andrews? Maybe her campaigning around the country gave her a taste for other places, other fights, or maybe she returned to live with her sister in Ipswich and continued her work locally.

A few years after the vote was won, a Roll of Honour was created to celebrate the women who went to prison for the cause.[2] Amongst the 1,100 or so names on the Roll are several of the women active in the Ipswich campaign: Constance Andrews, Hilda Birkett, Elizabeth Knight, Ethel Lowy, Grace Roe, Isabel Tippett and Florence Tunks. The name Margaret Fison also appears, but it has not been possible to ascertain whether this is the Ipswich WSPU member.

*The Vote* made this comment when suffrage was won:

To have won equal voting rights for women and men is a great victory, but it will be an infinitely greater achievement when we ... have decided that the whole wide world and all its opportunities is just as much the sphere of woman as of man.[3]

# APPENDIX ONE

# ABOUT THE LOCAL WOMEN

**CONSTANCE ANDREWS** was the main organiser of suffrage events in Ipswich. She was born in about 1864 in Stowmarket, and was a social reformer over many years. She lived with her sister, Lilla Pratt, and brother-in-law George at No. 160 Norwich Road, Ipswich. She became involved in suffrage politics in 1907 as secretary of the Ipswich and County Women's Suffrage Society, and founded the Ipswich branch of the more militant Women's Freedom League (WFL) in 1909. Constance organised an event at the Old Museum Rooms in Ipswich, where on census night 1911 about twenty-five women stayed up all night to avoid having to fill in their census schedule, as part of a 'No Vote, No Census' campaign. Her personal details do not appear on her household's census schedule. Later that year, she was said to be the first woman to go to prison for refusing to buy a dog licence, as part of the Tax Resistance campaign.

In 1912, she was voted onto the National Executive of the WFL, and campaigned for votes for women throughout the country.

**CATHERINE BASTIAN** supported suffrage events in Ipswich, and was part of the small group of active WFL women in the area. She formed a branch of the WFL in 1910 in Hadleigh. She lived at Fern Bank, No. 19 Gallows Hill, Hadleigh with her supportive husband, Jacob Henry Bastian. Both of them were at the Old Museum Rooms on the night of the census in 1911, and they did not complete their census schedule.

**MISS BLOCK** became a member of the Ipswich branch of the Women's Social and Political Union (WSPU) in 1910, and attended the London suffrage procession in June of that year with the Ipswich WSPU group.

**MISS BOBBY** had a confectioner's shop at No. 22 Queen Street, Ipswich. In 1912 some or all of this shop was leased to the WFL, and from here they sold suffrage literature and their magazine *The Vote*. Miss Bobby attended many WFL events at this time.

**BESS BOYD-BROWN** was a friend of Constance Andrews and was there when Constance was released from prison. She also accompanied her at the Women's Coronation Procession in London in June 1911. There are no contemporary records of her, but in 1983 she gave an interview to Nan Kerr (who was gathering material for the play *Women and Bits o' Boys* by Anthony Tuckey), when she shared her memories of Constance.

**MISS BYFORD** was a supporter of the WSPU from at least 1911. In March of that year, she spoke at an Independent Labour Party meeting in Ipswich, and urged Ipswich's MPs to pass women's suffrage into law (in order to avoid census evasion and resistance). She was still supporting WSPU events in Ipswich in 1914.

**LAURA CAY** was a longstanding supporter of women's suffrage, joining the new Ipswich WFL in May 1909. When the Ipswich branch of the WSPU was formed, she began to work within that organisation, speaking at their meetings and arranging events. At the time of the census in 1911, Laura was 36 years old and lived with her widowed mother at The Garth, Constitution Hill, Ipswich. She was still supporting the group in 1914.

**LADY MARY CAYLEY** lived at Tempe, Woodbridge, and was a supporter of suffrage from 1910, when she was in her late 40s. It is not entirely clear which organisation she worked within. She joined the WSPU Ipswich delegation on the London Procession of 1910, and hosted a visit from Mrs Pethwick-Lawrence in 1911. However, in 1913, when the Suffolk Pilgrimage came through East Suffolk, she was reported to be the president of the Woodbridge branch of the National Union of Women's Suffrage Societies.

**PHYLLIS CORNELL** appears to have been a WSPU supporter, who went up to London and joined in their window-smashing campaigns. We know this because she talked about her involvement in an interview by the *East Anglian Daily Times* in 1958. There is no contemporary record of her.

**LILLIAN CRANFIELD** lived at The Cottage, Burstall, and became a WSPU supporter from 1910. She hosted meetings in her village and in Ipswich with national suffragettes such as Maria Brackenbury and Constance Lytton.

She was part of the Ipswich WSPU contingent at the London Procession of June 1910.

**MRS CULLINGHAM** was the vice-president of the Ipswich and County Women's Suffrage Society in 1907, and was the daughter of the Ipswich MP, Mr Everett.

**MRS DE CANDOLE** was a supporter of the WFL. She appeared in the Pageant of Great Women in Ipswich in 1910, spoke at local WFL meetings in 1913, and was also part of a group who met the women on the Suffrage Pilgrimage as they came into Ipswich in the same year.

**MAUD DOWNING** was a local actress, who lent her support to the dramatic performances that the suffrage organisations put on. She appeared in the Pageant of Great Women in 1910, in the Hippodrome WFL plays in 1911 and then with the WSPU at the Felixstowe Exhibition in 1912.

**MISS ELVEY** was a strong suffrage supporter and joined the WSPU in 1910. She attended the Women's Procession in 1910 as part of the Ipswich WSPU group and was at the census evasion action at the Old Museum Rooms in April 1911. Her name is often associated with the organisation of events, right up to 1914.

**MARGARET FISON** was a strong supporter of the WSPU from 1910. She lived at Broad View, Constitution Hill, with her brother and two sisters. She attended the 1910 Women's Procession with the Ipswich group and was at the census evasion action at Ipswich's Old Museum Rooms in 1911. Her details do not appear on her household's census schedule. She was an artistic woman, and prepared all the posters for the suffrage plays put on at the Lyceum in 1911. In 1912 she created a poster/cartoon for the WSPU stall at the Felixstowe Exhibition called 'Anti-Suffrage Ostrich'. She was still active in 1914. The name appears on the Roll of Honour of Suffragette Prisoners 1905–14, but no record has been found locally of her imprisonment.

**SOPHIE FLEAR** was the headmistress of the Girls' High School in Ipswich and a long-standing suffragist. She was a committee member of Ipswich and County Women's Suffrage Society from 1907 and an active member of the Liberal Party. At the end of 1909 she proposed jointly with Conservative

Lillie Roe that women should withdraw their support and hard work from the political parties until they were able to vote.

**MRS FOSTER** was the secretary of the WFL group at Woolpit. She lived at Lawn Farm in the village. Her group held meetings in the nearby villages, and they also prepared knitted items for sale in the WFL shop in Ipswich.

**MISS GARDNER** was a member of the Ipswich and County Women's Suffrage Society, and had become its secretary by 1913. She lived at No. 73 Foxhall Road. In 1913 she met the Suffrage Pilgrimage as it came into Ipswich.

**MRS GARNER** supported the Ipswich branch of the WFL from 1909, helping with the organisation of many events and going to London with other group members to the Women's Procession of 1910. In 1912 she became a committee member, and continued to work with the group over the next years.

**MRS W.T. GRIFFITHS** was a committee member of the Ipswich and County Women's Suffrage Society in 1907, and was a Liberal. She was present at many meetings of this group and met the Suffrage Pilgrimage in 1913 as it came into Ipswich.

**HARRIETT GRIMWADE** was the chairwoman of the first Ipswich and County Women's Suffrage Society when it set up in 1871, holding that position for a year. She lived at Norton House, Henley Road, Ipswich, and went on to do philanthropic work in the town. She founded and ran an orphanage at Hope House, Foxhall Road, Ipswich for many years.

**MISS HARRISON** was headmistress of the Girls' Municipal Secondary School, and a committee member of the Ipswich and County Women's Suffrage Society in 1907. She met the Suffrage Pilgrimage in 1913 as it came into Ipswich.

**MRS HOSSACK** was one of the most long-standing of all the Ipswich suffragettes. She lived at No. 49 Berners Street, Ipswich with her supportive husband James, a consultant at the East Suffolk and Ipswich Hospital, and their three children. She was the secretary of the Ipswich and County Women's Suffrage Society before Constance Andrews took over that role in 1907, and then moved with Constance to the WFL when the Ipswich branch formed in 1909. There was hardly an event over the next few years that she was not at, usually helping with the organisation, and speaking at many meetings. She was at the census evasion event at the Old Museum Rooms in April 1911, and her personal details are not included in her household's schedule. She became honorary secretary of the Ipswich WFL in 1913 after Constance Andrews moved to take up national suffrage work, and she was staunch and persistent during the unpleasant events of the 1914 by-election.

**MISS HOWARD** was a member of the committee of the Ipswich and County Women's Suffrage Society in 1907, but became a member of the WFL in 1910. She was a big seller of the WFL newspaper *The Vote*, and became branch treasurer in 1911. In the summer of 1913, she and Lilla Pratt joined Constance Andrews on her WFL campaign in Devon. She was part of the difficult by-election campaign in 1914.

**MRS HUTLEY** was a member of the Ipswich WFL from 1909, and in the next year became assistant treasurer of the branch. She was a regular speaker at the group's meetings and was still a committee member in 1913.

**MRS JOSLING** was the secretary of the Stowmarket group of WFL members. She lived at No. 59 Limetree Place, Stowmarket.

**MISS KENNETT** was president of the Ipswich and County Women's Suffrage Society in 1907. She may have changed to the WSPU, as she is recorded as being part of the WSPU group that went to the 1910 Women's Coronation Procession in London.

**EVELYN SPENCER KING** was best known as co-ordinator of the WSPU shop, which was first at No. 4a Princes Street before moving to No. 2 Dial Lane in 1911 and No. 6 Tower Street in 1913. She supported many of the group's events and activities, and by 1913 was honorary secretary of the Ipswich branch, after Grace Roe had returned to do suffrage work in London. She lived at No. 24 Russell Road, Ipswich with her widowed father. Her details do not appear on her household's 1911 census schedule.

**HORTENSE MARY LANE** lived in 1909 at Whitton Street in Ipswich, and then at Cowslip Dairy Farm, Witnesham, with her supportive husband Frank Lane. She was the first and most persistent of the Ipswich suffragettes to take action under the Tax Resistance campaign, first appearing in court in 1909 for refusing to pay her Inhabited House Duty. She repeated tax resistance offences (normally refusing to buy a dog licence) almost every year up to and including 1914 with her friend from London, Dr Elizabeth Knight. She always refused to pay her fine, and bailiffs took goods and auctioned them to meet the debt. Often their farm waggon was used for this purpose, gaining a certain amount of fame in its own right! The suffragettes used these occasions to hold meetings and gain maximum publicity. Hortense often helped with WFL events in Ipswich, and helped to sell *The Vote*. She did not evade the 1911 census, and her schedule shows her to be 34 years old at that time with two small children.

**ETHEL LOWY** was a WSPU supporter who came from London to Felixstowe in 1912, possibly to support Grace Roe in organising in this area. She lived at Woodcroft, Bath Road, Felixstowe. She was a member of a large WSPU-supporting family in London, several of whom had been to prison whilst campaigning for the vote. Ethel herself served one week in prison for breaking windows in London in 1911. She tried to organise a WSPU group in Felixstowe. After 1913, she helped with national events, including the funeral of Emily Wilding Davison.

**MRS MCCRERY** was a long-term supporter of the WFL, helping at events from 1909. In 1912 she became a committee member of the local branch. She was one of the women who met Constance Andrews out of prison in 1911.

**ADA MATTHEW** was the secretary of the Hadleigh branch of the WFL, and lived with her elderly mother at No. 21 Fir Terrace – next door to WFL stalwarts Mr and Mrs Bastian. Her 1911 census schedule shows her to be 39 years old.

**ALICE MAYHEW** was a singer who was associated with Constance Andrews' brother-in-law George Pratt, a music teacher. She appears in several press reports in 1911 as the singer of 'The Awakening', the new WFL 'anthem'. She sang this song at many WFL meetings; including the public meeting the night before the census evasion at the Old Museum Rooms when the reporter wrote that she 'has a rich, well-trained alto voice'. We know that the women evading the census in the Old Museum Rooms sang 'The Awakening', but it is not reported whether Alice Mayhew was there to lead it.

**MISS MILANO** lived at St Michael's, Cornwall Rd, Felixstowe and was a member of the Ipswich WFL from 1910. She supported and assisted at many WFL events in Ipswich and Felixstowe.

**ELLEN CONSTANCE NORMAN** lived at Brantham Court, Brantham, near Manningtree with her husband Charles Kensitt Norman JP, and parents-in-law. The whole family were suffrage supporters and Ellen Norman hosted and presided over many suffrage meetings. It was at her house, in 1909, that Constance Andrews declared that she would start an Ipswich branch of the WFL, but from 1910 Ellen Norman supported the WSPU. The household's 1911 census form shows that she was aged 39, born in Southern Australia and had only recently married.

**PHYLLIS PEARCE** lived at Morecombe House at No. 55 Henley Rd in Ipswich. She was a WSPU member from 1910, hosting meetings and attending the Women's Coronation Procession in June of that year with the Ipswich group. She acted in the 1910 Pageant of Great Women, organised by the WFL locally. She lived with her parents and brother, and her details do not appear on the household's census schedule.

**MRS PICKFORD** who lived in the Buttermarket, was the secretary of the Ipswich and County Women's Suffrage Society from 1872.

**EDITH PLACE** lived at No. 34 Quilter Road, Felixstowe, and from 1912 was the secretary of the Walton and District branch of the NUWSS. In 1913, she was one of a large group of women who met the NUWSS Suffrage Pilgrimage as it came into Ipswich.

**MISS POLLITT** was a WSPU supporter from 1910 and went to the Coronation Procession of that year with the Ipswich women. Later that same year, she presented Emmeline Pankhurst with a bouquet when she spoke at a meeting in Ipswich. She helped organise the WSPU events at the Felixstowe exhibition in 1911.

**LILLA PRATT** was Constance Andrews' younger sister, and a committed suffragette in her own right. She lived with her husband, George Pratt, and two sons at No. 160 Norwich Road, Ipswich, and gave a home to Constance. Lilla was part of the campaign alongside Constance, becoming a member of the Ipswich and County Women's Suffrage Society committee in 1907, and then of the WFL when it formed in 1909. She became secretary of the Ipswich WFL in 1913 when Constance took on responsibilities with the national campaign. Throughout the years she was present at, helped organise and supported almost every WFL event in the town. In 1911, she evaded the census, and later in the year, took food into Ipswich prison daily for Constance who was serving a week's sentence. Her husband, George Pratt, a music teacher, was also committed to the cause. He provided music support to the Pageant of Great Women in 1910, and other events.

**MRS DOUGLAS REID** lived at Henley Hall, Ipswich and was a supporter of the WSPU from 1910, attending the Women's Coronation Procession in that year. She hosted many WSPU meetings, including when Mrs Pethwick-Lawrence came to Ipswich to speak in 1911.

**ADA RIDLEY** was firstly a WFL supporter, and went to the auction of Hortense Lane's goods in 1909, but joined the WSPU in 1910. She was still supporting local actions in 1914. She sewed a banner for the Ipswich WSPU for the 1910 London Women's Coronation Procession, with the words 'Be Just and Fear Not'.

**BESSIE RIDLEY** Ada's sister, was a committee member in 1907 of the Ipswich and County Women's Suffrage Society, and later joined the WSPU. She supported WSPU events in Ipswich over several years.

**GRACE ROE** of the WSPU, was sent to Ipswich in 1910 to start a branch here, and organised many meetings and events, getting financial and other support from influential women of the area. She lodged at No. 19 Silent Street, Ipswich, and arranged for many significant national suffragettes to come and speak in the town. In 1913, she was drawn back to London to manage the WSPU as its leaders were in prison.

**LILLIE ROE** was about 50 years old when she joined the Ipswich WSPU in 1910, and she was active in the organisation and support of many events. She had joined the Ipswich and Country Women's Suffrage Society in 1907, and later often appeared at WFL events. She lived with her mother at No. 55 Fonnereau Road, Ipswich. Lillie Roe wrote in the paper that she had been part of the 1911 census evasion events, but her details appear on her household's census schedule.

**HEPHZIBAH STANSFIELD** was a committed suffrage supporter from 1908, supporting many WFL events, and becoming a member of the committee in 1912. She was very involved in the arrangements in the run-up to the census evasion event of 1911, but, in fact, her census schedule shows that she did complete her details. In 1910, at the age of 37, she married Herbert Henry Stansfield, and they lived at the Old Mill House, Witnesham. He was an art teacher at Ipswich School of Art, and a staunch supporter of women's suffrage. As early as 1908 he was hoping to form an Ipswich branch of the Men's Franchise League.

**MISS M.L. STEWARD** lived at Graham House, Graham Road, Ipswich and in 1913 was the secretary of the Ipswich branch of the Church League for Women's Suffrage.

**ISABEL TIPPETT** was one of the most prominent suffragettes in the Ipswich area, speaking at countless WFL meetings and organising and supporting events. She lived with her husband and two small children (one of whom would become the composer Michael Tippett) at The Cottage, Park Road, Wetherden, and supported the Ipswich, Hadleigh and Woolpit branches. She was a cousin of WFL President, Charlotte Despard. A novelist and playwright, she wrote sketches and short plays which were performed at WFL events. She was a key organiser of the 1911 census evasion event, presiding at the public meetings in Bury and Ipswich at which Laurence Housman explained the action that was being taken, and neither her own, nor her husband Henry's, details seem to be on their household's census schedule. She may have had an eccentric appearance as, on 19 May 1911, the *East Anglian Daily Times* reporter said she 'attracted attention by her flowing but abbreviated costume ... Her robe was difficult to describe – somewhere between the robe of Portia and that of a nurse'. In 1912, she was fined for not having a dog licence, as part of the WFL Tax Resistance campaign. She was said to be a strong speaker, who eventually overcame any opposition in the crowd, and worked persistently for the cause during the difficult by-election campaign of 1914. She started to do more work for the National WFL in 1913, travelling the country to support local branches.

# APPENDIX TWO

# THE MAIN SUFFRAGE ORGANISATIONS

## The Actresses' Franchise League (AFL)

The AFL was formed in 1908 and had as its president the famous Shakespearean actress, Ellen Terry. Her daughter, Edith Craig, was its director. In a male-dominated profession, its aim was to promote equality for actresses. It also worked for the enfranchisement of women through the message of its plays, and was available to support all the main national and local suffrage organisations. By 1912, they had about 750 members, which included most prominent actresses of the day.

There was an increasing demand for suffrage entertainments, as these were seen as a popular way of putting the message across, and also for local groups to have a joint activity and a lot of fun. Playwrights began to write specific propaganda material which was performed to high production standards across the country by professional actresses, often working with local suffragettes.

The AFL was closely linked with other artists' organisations – for example, the Women Writers' Suffrage League, the Musicians' Suffrage League and the Artists' Suffrage League.

As well as performing plays, AFL members trained fellow suffragettes in public speaking, holding debates, opening fundraising events and the use of make-up and disguise to avoid police arrest.

The AFL came to the Ipswich area on at least three occasions to perform their plays and help with public events.

# National Union of Women's Suffrage Societies (NUWSS)

Formed towards the end of the nineteenth century this society served as an umbrella organisation for the many groups springing up in towns around the country. Millicent Fawcett (one of the Suffolk Garrett family, and younger sister of Elizabeth Garrett Anderson) was its president. It was an organisation which lobbied for constitutional reform for women's suffrage, and did not support its sister organisations in their more militant actions.

By 1914 it had 480 branches with 53,000 members, and was by far the largest suffrage organisation. The Ipswich and County Women's Suffrage Society never formally affiliated to the NUWSS, but its politics and strategy were similar. There were branches in several small Suffolk towns.

The NUWSS newspaper was *The Common Cause*, which started in 1909. Its colours were red, green and white.

# Women's Freedom League (WFL)

The WFL formed in 1907 under the leadership of Charlotte Despard when several prominent members of the Women's Social and Political Union broke away in protest at the authoritarian nature of the Pankhurst leadership. They were not opposed to militancy and participated in a number of WSPU initiatives with many members going to prison as a result of their protests. However, they did not agree with the destruction of property that featured in WSPU actions later in the campaign. The WFL motto was 'Dare to be Free'. They worked closely with the Women's Tax Resistance League on the 'No Vote, No Tax' and 'No Vote, No Census' campaigns.

The WFL always concerned itself with a broad range of women's issues, and felt it important to give women training, experience and confidence for wider participation in politics and public life.

The WFL was the main suffrage organisation in Ipswich, with Constance Andrews and a close group of women leading action in this area.

Their national magazine was *The Vote*, which started in 1909, and their colours were green, gold and white.

# Women's Tax Resistance League (WTRL)

The WTRL was formed in 1909 to explore how women might resist paying tax as part of the suffrage campaign. The group was closely associated with the WFL and advised women on how they could evade paying income and other taxes. Many women preferred to resist paying one-off taxes such as dog and carriage licences, because this carried greater possibilities for publicity.

In 1911 the league became interested in the 'No Vote, No Census' action of the WFL, and because they had built up expertise regarding the legal situation in tax resistance, they provided legal advice about census resistance and evasion.

Several local women were tax resisters – Hortense Lane, Constance Andrews and Isabel Tippett were all prosecuted for not purchasing dog licences, and Constance Andrews went to prison as a result.

# Women's Social and Political Union (WSPU)

The WSPU was formed in 1903 by Emmeline Pankhurst and her three daughters, Christabel, Sylvia and Adela. They had been campaigning for women's suffrage for some time, but felt that constitutional methods were having no result. As a result 'Deeds not words' was their motto. The WSPU instigated actions of all kinds – huge colourful processions, exhibitions, deputations to parliament and the prime minister. When it became clear that the government was unsympathetic, they began to use civil disobedience and militancy on an increasing scale to achieve their aims.

A local branch of the WSPU was formed in 1909 by Grace Roe, who came to live in Ipswich to lead the campaign.

Their national magazines were *Votes for Women*, and later *The Suffragette*. Their colours were purple, green and white.

# NOTES

## Chapter 1
## The Ladies' Petition 1866

1 Arthur F.J. Brown, *Chartist Movement in Essex and Suffolk* (University of Essex, 1979), p. 5.

2 John Stuart Mill wrote *The Subjection of Women* in 1869 and continued to fight for equality for women. Henry Fawcett later married Millicent Garrett, who became leader of the National Union of Women's Suffrage Societies at the end of the century.

3 Ann Dingsdale, *'Generous and Lofty Sympathies': The Kensington Society, the 1866 women's suffrage petition and the development of mid-Victorian feminism,* unpublished thesis (University of Greenwich, 1995), p. 126.

4 *Ibid.,* p. 10.

5 Copies of The Ladies' Petition are contained within Collections at Girton College, Cambridge. I am grateful to the College Library for enabling me to study the Petition and other relevant works of that time.

6 I am grateful to Ann Dingsdale for generously sharing with me her research on the signatories from Suffolk.

7 Elizabeth Crawford, *The Women's Suffrage Movement in Britain and Ireland: A Regional Survey* (London, 2005), pp. 85–87.

8 Postal and Commercial Directory of Suffolk 1864 (London, 1864), p. 227.

9 *Ibid.,* p. 239.

10 A.C. Hyde and N.G. Perkins, *Westerfield Church and Village 1087–1987* (Suffolk, 1987), p. 174.

11 Joyce Marlow (ed.), *Votes for Women: The Virago Book of Suffragettes* (London, 2001), p. 11.

12 Jo Manton, *Elizabeth Garrett Anderson* (London, 1987), p. 13.

13 Marlow (ed.), *Votes for Women,* p. 13.

14 Diane Atkinson, *Suffragettes in Pictures* (Sutton Publishing, 1996), p. xv.

15 *Suffolk Chronicle*, 26 February 1870.

16 *Ibid.*, 15 April 1871.

# Chapter 2
## Stirring Up Ipswich

1 Much of the information about Stowmarket as it was at that time comes from Mike Durrant, *Stowmarket Then and Now* (Stowmarket, 2003); and Harry Double, *Stowmarket – A Pageant in Pictures* (Stowmarket, 2002).

2 Correspondence between Constance Andrews and Mrs Stanbury, and with Philippa Strachey of the London Society for Women's Suffrage, is held in collections at the Women's Library, London. This refers to a letter from Constance Andrews to Mrs Stanbury, 24 March 1907.

3 Letter from Constance Andrews to Philippa Strachey, 22 February 1907.

4 Letter from Constance Andrews to Mrs Stanbury, 24 March 1907.

5 Letter from Constance Andrews to Philippa Strachey, 23 April 1907.

6 Letter from Constance Andrews to Philippa Strachey, 4 July 1907.

7 Letter from Philippa Strachey to Constance Andrews, 6 July 1907.

8 *The Women's Franchise*, 12 September 1907.

9 *Evening Star*, 26 March 1908.

10 Lisa Tickner, *The Spectacle of Women: Imagery of the Women's Campaign 1907–1914* (Chicago 1988) p. 81.

11 *Ibid.*, p. 67.

12 Robert Radcliffe, *History of the Working Class Movement in Ipswich 1900–1918*, Vol. II (1953), p. 33.

13 *Ibid.*, p. 28.

14 *Evening Star*, 25 October 1907.

15 *Votes for Women*, 3 December 1908.

# Chapter 3
## Hope and Disappointment

1 *Evening Star*, 29 May 1909.

2 *Suffolk Chronicle*, 4 June 1909.

3 Events of 28 May 1909 are reported in *Evening Star*, 29 May 1909, and *The Women's Franchise*, 3 June 1909.

4 Jill Liddington, *Rebel Girls* (London, 2006), p. 208.

5 Quoted in Midge Mackenzie, *Shoulder to Shoulder: A Documentary* (London: Penguin, 1985), p. 109.

6   *Ibid.*, p. 126.

7   The First World War prevented any study of the long-term effects of forcible feeding. The balance of opinion after the suffrage campaign was that it was medically unethical to feed someone against their will. In 1975, the World Medical Association banned it in the Declaration of Tokyo.

8   Reported in *East Anglian Daily Times* (hereafter *EADT*), 22 July 1909 and *The Women's Franchise*, 29 July 1909.

9   *Votes for Women*, 4 February 1910.

10  *The Common Cause*, 31 January 1910.

11  *EADT*, 6 May 1910.

12  *The Vote*, 28 May 1910.

13  *Votes for Women*, 3 June 1910.

14  *EADT*, 20 June 1910.

15  *EADT*, 19 July 1910.

# Chapter 4
## 'No Vote, No Census'

1   *The Vote*, 11 February 1911.

2   Jill Liddington and Elizabeth Crawford, '"Women do not count, neither shall they be counted": Suffrage, Citizenship and the Battle for the 1911 Census' in *History Workshop Journal*, Issue 71. I am grateful to Jill Liddington for also generously sharing with me the research and ideas which lie behind this article.

3   *The Times*, 14 February 1911.

4   *Votes for Women*, 31 March 1911 reports that Ipswich ILP passed a motion at a recent meeting recommending that Ipswich's two MPs should do whatever they could to ensure that the government gave time to the Conciliation Bill.

5   *Evening Star*, 17 March 1911.

6   *The Vote*, 1 April 1911.

7   *Evening Star*, 31 March 1911.

8   *The Vote*, 1 April 1911.

9   *Votes for Women*, 21 April 1911.

10  *Ibid.*, 7 April 1911.

11  *The Vote*, 8 April 1911.

12  *Votes for Women*, 7 April 1911.

13  Kelly's Directory of Ipswich 1906 (London, 1906), p. 189 and Kelly's Directory of Ipswich 1912 (London, 1912), p. 202, list Herbert Edward Archer at this property.

14  *EADT*, 2 April 1911.

15  Enumerator's Summary Book of households in Museum Street, Ipswich, Census 1911 (National Archives).

16  *Suffolk Chronicle*, 7 April 1911.

17  *EADT*, 4 April 1911.

18  *The Vote*, 15 April 1911.

19  *Evening Star*, 3 April 1911.

20  *Votes for Women*, 24 March 1911.

21  *Suffolk Chronicle*, 7 April 1911.

22  Liddington and Crawford in *History Workshop Journal*, Issue 71, pp. 116–19.

23  *Suffolk Chronicle*, 7 April 1911.

24  *Votes for Women*, 21 April 1911, lists Evelyn King, Margaret Fison and Miss Elvey as being at the Old Museum Rooms on census night.

25  Liddington and Crawford in *History Workshop Journal*, Issue 71, p. 126, endnote 69.

26  *Votes for Women*, 15 April 1911.

## Chapter 5
## The Busy Year Continues

1  The report of the court case under the heading 'No Vote, No Tax' is in the *EADT*, 21 April 1911.

2  *EADT*, 19 May 1911.

3  The Criminal Register, Ipswich, 1908–1921 is held in the Suffolk Record Office.

4  *EADT*, 22 May 1911.

5  Reports of the celebrations on Constance Andrews' discharge from prison are in the *Evening Star*, 26 May 1911.

6  From an unpublished interview with Bess Boyd-Brown by Nan Kerr in her research for the play *All Women an' Bits o' Boys* – compiled and directed by Anthony Tuckey at the Wolsey Theatre, Ipswich in 1983. Warm thanks to Nan Kerr for allowing me to quote from this interview.

7  *Evening Star*, 26 May 1911.

8  Susan Croft (ed.), *Votes for Women and Other Plays* (London: Aurora Metro Press, 2009), p. 167.

9  H. Arncliffe-Sennett, *An Englishwoman's Home* (London, 1910), is held in collections at The Women's Library at the LSE, London.

10  The report of the Lyceum performances is in *EADT*, 11 May 1911.

11  A sketch by Isabel Tippett called *The Stuff that 'Eroes are made of* was printed in *The Vote*, 19 August 1911, and is her only stage work to have come to light at present.

12  *EADT*, 30 June 1911.

13  From an unpublished interview with Bess Boyd-Brown by Nan Kerr in her research for the play *All Women an' Bits o' Boys*. Bess Boyd-Brown tells various anecdotes about the activities of Constance Andrews, including this insight into the Pratt/Andrews' household: 'The sister was a vegetarian, and Miss Andrews was ... but he [George Pratt] wasn't. One night he came out and he used to wear a long coat like Sherlock Holmes and we followed him down the little streets, and he went to a little shop where they sell pies ... we started to giggle, and I said: "Well, he's not a vegetarian!" He went in and bought this pie. I suppose his wife wouldn't have it in the house!'

14  Michael Tippett, *Those Twentieth Century Blues* (London, 1991), p. 3.

15  *EADT*, 12 July 1958. No contemporary record of Phyllis Cornell's suffrage activities has been found.


# Chapter 6
## And Still No Vote

1  Constance Andrews' activities as a national campaigner can be traced through the minutes of the National Executive of the Women's Freedom League 1912–14, held in collections at The Women's Library.

2  Antonia Raeburn, *Militant Suffragettes* (London, 1984), p. 183.

3  Reports in *EADT*, 9 and 10 May 1912.

4  Reports in *EADT*, 8 July 1912, and in *Votes for Women*, 12 July 1912.

5  *Votes for Women*, 12 July 1912.

6  *EADT*, 21 April 1912.

7  *The Vote*, 21 September 1912.

8  Kelly's Directory of Ipswich 1912 (London, 1912).

9  *The Vote*, 17 August 1912.

10  *Ibid.*, 13 July 1912.

11  *Evening Star*, 12 February 1913.

12  *Woodbridge Reporter and Wickham Market Gazette*, 19 June 1913.

13  *EADT*, 16 July 1913.

14  *Ibid.*, 17 July 1913.

15  *Ibid.*, 18 July 1913.

16  *Evening Star*, 4 October 1913.

17  *Evening Star*, 3 February 1914.

18  *The Suffragette*, 27 March 1914.

19  *The Vote*, 10 April 1914.

## Chapter 7
## A Final, Local Militant Act

1  Wayne Bennett, *Felixstowe's Last Bath Night* (Felixstowe, 2002), pp. 6–19. Using press reports and the diary, Mr Bennett has put together a chronology of the movements of the two women on the days up to and including the arson attacks.

2  The different sightings of the two women on this night are recorded in the newspaper reports of the evidence given at their trial. *EADT*, 16 May 1914.

3  The events in this paragraph are related in *The Suffragette*, 8 May 1914.

4  *Suffolk Chronicle*, 8 May 1914.

5  The events of this day were reported in *EADT*, 16 May 1914.

6  *Ibid.*

7  *The Suffragette*, 15 May 1914.

8  *The Vote*, 29 May 1914.

9  Constance Andrews is not mentioned in any of these reports, and we can only assume that she was engaged in WFL work in other parts of the country. She spent the summer on the Isle of Man, where women had had the vote since 1880, talking to holidaymakers from all over Britain about suffrage.

10  *The Suffragette*, 13 March 1914.

11  Letter from Mr Woolnough, curator of Ipswich Museum and Free Library, 23 June 1914. This passage is used courtesy of Colchester and Ipswich Museum Service, Colchester Museum Collection.

12  *The Bury Post*, 8 June 1914.

13  *Evening Star*, 19 June 1914.

14  In *The Suffragette*, 1 May 1914, Dr Moxon wrote about tests he had carried out on the urine of forcibly fed women on their discharge from prison. They revealed that women were being given a 'chemical restraint' of bromine. The effect would be to make the mind abnormally dulled and unresponsive, and it could lead to permanent mental breakdown.

15  Antonia Raeburn, *Militant Suffragettes* (London, 1974), p. 251.

16  *The Suffragette*, 7 August 1914.

17  Wayne Bennett, *Felixstowe's Last Bath Night* (Felixstowe, 2002), p. 65.

## Afterword

1 V. Irene Cockcroft, *New Dawn Women: Women in the Arts and Crafts and Suffrage Movements at the Dawn of the Twentieth Century* (London, 2005), p. 38.

2 *The Roll of Honour- Suffragette Prisoners 1905–1914* is in collections at The Women's Library. There is no publication date, but it is thought to have been compiled in the 1950s.

3 *The Vote*, 6 July 1928.

# BIBLIOGRAPHY

## Primary Sources

### Journals

*The Bury Post*, 1914
*The Common Cause*, 1910
*Daily Sketch*, 1911
*East Anglian Daily Times*, 1909–14
*Evening Star* [Ipswich's local newspaper], 1907–14
*The Manchester Guardian*, 1911
*Suffolk Chronicle*, 1870–1914
*The Suffragette*, 1914
*The Times*, 1911
*The Vote*, 1909–28
*Votes for Women*, 1908–28
*The Women's Franchise*, 1907–09
*Women's Suffrage Journal*, 1871
*Woodbridge Reporter and Wickham Market Gazette*, 1913

### Other

Census Records, 1861, 1871, 1881, 1891, 1901, 1911 (National Archives)
Constance Andrews' letters (Women's Library at LSE Collections)
Criminal Register, Ipswich, 1908–20 (Suffolk Record Office)
Interview of Bess Boyd-Brown with Nan Kerr, 1983, transcript
Ladies' Petition 1866 (Copies in Collections at Girton College, Cambridge)
Minutes of the Women's Freedom League National Executive 1912–14
   (Women's Library at LSE Collections)
Postal and Commercial Directory of Suffolk 1864 (London, 1864)
Kelly's Directory of Ipswich 1906, 1910, 1912

# Secondary Sources

Arncliffe-Sennett, H., *An Englishwoman's Home* (London: Actresses' Franchise League, 1910)

Atkinson, Diane, *The Suffragettes in Pictures* (Stroud: Sutton Publishing, 1996)

Bennett, Wayne, *Felixstowe's Last Bath Night* (Felixstowe, 2002)

Cockcroft, Irene and Susan Croft, *Art, Theatre and Women's Suffrage* (London: Aurora Metro Press, 2010)

Crawford, Elizabeth, *Enterprising Women: The Garretts and Their Circle* (London: Francis Boutle, 2002)

Crawford, Elizabeth, *The Women's Suffragette Movement in Britain and Ireland: A Regional Survey* (London: Routledge, 2005)

Crawford, Elizabeth, *Women's Suffrage Movement, A Reference Guide 1866–1928* (London: Routledge, 2001)

Croft, Susan (ed.), *Votes for Women and Other Plays* (London: Aurora Metro Press, 2009)

Dingsdale, Ann, *'Generous and Lofty Sympathies': The Kensington Society, the 1866 women's suffrage petition and the development of mid-Victorian feminism*, unpublished thesis (University of Greenwich, 1995)

Eustance, Claire, Joan Ryan and Laura Ugolini, *A Suffrage Reader: Charting Directions in British Suffrage History* (London: Leicester University Press, 2000)

Holledge, Julie, *Innocent Flowers: Women in the Edwardian Theatre* (London: Virago, 1981)

Joannou, Maroula and June Purvis (eds), *The Women's Suffrage Movement: New Feminist Perspectives* (Manchester: Manchester University Press 1998)

Liddington, Jill, *Rebel Girls: Their Fight for the Vote* (London: Virago, 2006)

Liddington, Jill and Elizabeth Crawford, '"Women do not count, neither shall they be counted": Suffrage, Citizenship and the Battle for the 1911 Census' in *History Workshop Journal*, Issue 71.

Marlow, Joyce, *Votes for Women: The Virago Book of Suffragettes* (London: Virago, 2000)

Mackenzie, Midge, *Shoulder to Shoulder: A Documentary* (London: Penguin, 1985)

People's History Museum, *Battle for the Ballot*, (Manchester, 2007)

A.J.R. *Suffrage Annual and Women's Who's Who 1913* (London: Stanley Paul, 1913)

Raeburn, Antonia, *Militant Suffragettes* (London: New English Library, 1974)

Ratcliffe, Robert, *History of the Working Class Movement in Ipswich 1900–1908*, Vol. II (Author, 1953)

Suffrage Fellowship England, *Roll of Honour: Suffragette Prisoners 1905–1914* (London, *c.* 1950)

Tickner, Lisa, *The Spectacle of Women: Imagery of the Suffragette Campaign* (Chicago: University of Chicago, 1988)

Also from The History Press

# CELEBRATING
# WOMEN'S HISTORY

Find these titles and more at
**www.thehistorypress.co.uk**

The History Press

Also from The History Press

# SUFFOLK

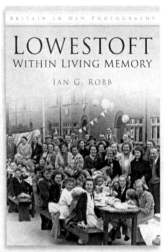

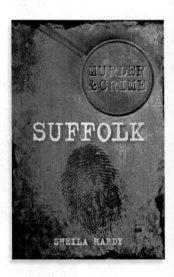

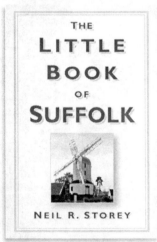

Find these titles and more at
**www.thehistorypress.co.uk**

The History Press

Also from The History Press

# GREAT WAR BRITAIN

Great War Britain is a unique new local series to mark the centenary of the Great War. In partnership with archives and museums across Great Britain, the series provides an evocative portrayal of life during this 'war to end all wars'. In a scrapbook style, and beautifully illustrated, it includes features such as personal memoirs, letters home, diary extracts, newspaper reports, photographs, postcards and other local First World War ephemera.

Find these titles and more at
**www.thehistorypress.co.uk**